Praise for James Tate

"The poet of possibilities, of morph, of surprising consequences, lovely or disastrous. I return to Tate's books more often perhaps than to any others when I want to be reminded afresh of the possibilities of poetry."　　　　　　　　　　　　　　　　　—John Ashbery

"One of the most prolific and admired American poets. . . . Tate saw the world the way a short-story writer or a novelist would. . . . A complex vision, both dreamlike and real, banal, cruel, and with a sumptuous sense of our lives."　　—Charles Simic, *New York Review of Books*

"Quite a few generations of poets in the United States simply could not have found their voices without his guiding, mischievous, brilliant, darkly-lit spirit. . . . [He] had a front-row seat at the apocalypse before anyone else even knew that circus was coming to town."
　　　　　　　　　　　　　　　　　　　　—Jorie Graham

"There is nothing like being in a James Tate poem. To read one is to enter a world where anything can happen, be it terrifying, ridiculous, sublime, mundane, or impossibly tender. *Dome of the Hidden Pavilion* belongs among his finest work, and demonstrates yet again that he was surely one of our greatest American poets."
　　　　　　　　　　　　　　　　　　—Matthew Zapruder

"The rare American poet who managed to make poems that were at once fanciful and grave, mundane and transcendent. . . . A tonic, in his poems, for the chaos around us."　　　　　　—*New York Times*

"Among the strangest and most influential American poets of the past fifty years. . . . Quietly gregarious in the spirit of Emily Dickinson, awake to the crabbed beauty of his perceptions."
　　　　　　　　　　　　　　　　—Dan Chiasson, *The New Yorker*

DOME OF THE

HIDDEN PAVILION

ALSO BY JAMES TATE

POETRY

The Lost Pilot
The Oblivion Ha-Ha
Hints to Pilgrims
Absences
Viper Jazz
Riven Doggeries
Constant Defender
Reckoner
Distance from Loved Ones
Selected Poems
Worshipful Company of Fletchers
Shroud of the Gnome
Memoir of the Hawk
Return to the City of White Donkeys
The Ghost Soldiers
The Eternal Ones of the Dream

PROSE

The Route as Briefed
Dreams of a Robot Dancing Bee

DOME OF THE

HIDDEN PAVILION

New Poems

James Tate

ecco

An Imprint of HarperCollins *Publishers*

DOME OF THE HIDDEN PAVILION. Copyright © 2015 by James Tate. All rights reserved. Printed in the United States of America. No part of this book may be used or reproduced in any manner whatsoever without written permission except in the case of brief quotations embodied in critical articles and reviews. For information address HarperCollins Publishers, 195 Broadway, New York, NY 10007.

HarperCollins books may be purchased for educational, business, or sales promotional use. For information please e-mail the Special Markets Department at SPsales@harpercollins.com.

A hardcover edition of this book was published in 2015 by Ecco, an imprint of HarperCollins Publishers.

FIRST ECCO PAPERBACK EDITION PUBLISHED 2016.

Designed by Mary Austin Speaker

Library of Congress Cataloging-in-Publication Data has been applied for.

ISBN 978-0-06-239921-2

16 17 18 19 20   OV/RRD   10 9 8 7 6 5 4 3 2 1

For Emily,

with love and gratitude

contents

i.

ii.

iii.

acknowledgments

Jubilat, The Massachusetts Review, The New York Times, Notnostrums, Rain Taxi, Barnstorm Series, Yahoo! News

i.

Mr. Leaves

      I saw someone coming in the distance, but couldn't make out who it was. The closer they got the more blurred the face became. Until finally I saw it was just a whirlwind of leaves. It was only me on a football field walking toward the street with my handbag thrown over my shoulder with this big funnel of leaves coming toward me like a man. Then it passed me and went up on the street. And then it disappeared. I walked on, toward the bank where I had some business to do. A man appeared out of an alley and stopped me and said, "Did you see that man made out of leaves go by?" "I did, could have fooled me," I said. "Hey, do you suppose you could lend me a dollar for a cup of coffee?" "No, I can't. I'm on my way to the bank," I said. I left him there and went on my way. Pretty soon a little boy crossed my path. He stopped me in my path and said, "I know who you are. You're the Man-of-Leaves. You just took your coat off. You can't fool me." "You're a pretty smart fellow, but you're wrong this time," I said, and went on my way. When I got to the bank I went in and waited to see an officer. When I saw one was free I went in. In the chair behind the desk sat a pile of leaves. It said, "Can I help you?" I stumbled at first, but managed to say, "I'm looking for a small loan, a thousand dollars for, say, twelve months." "Of course. Would you like a 4½% or a 5½% loan?" it said. "I'd like the 4½% if you don't mind," I said. "Very good choice," it said. It made out the papers and handed them to me. "Have a nice day," it said. "It's windy out there," I said. "You're telling me," it said, smoothing himself with satisfaction.

A Largely Questioning Article Offering Few Answers

When Roberta came home from the hospital she had tears in her eyes. I grabbed her and kissed her. "What happened?" I said. "He died," she said. "Who died?" I said. "The doctor. When he entered Mother's room he was so startled he had a heart attack," she said. "I don't understand. What startled him?" I said. "Mother. She had grown nine feet tall, and her face is all contorted. She's really quite frightening," she said. "Isn't there anything they can do for her?" I said. "All the medicines they have given her are tearing her apart. They are anxious for her to die, but she seems to just keep getting stronger. They are at an utter loss of what to do next," she said. "Perhaps we should take her out of there," I said. "But she wouldn't really fit in this house, or any house I can think of," she said. "Perhaps we should just take her out into the wild and let her go," I said. Roberta went silent and started fidgeting about the kitchen. She put away dishes and mopped the counter. I said, "Roberta?" And she said, "I'm thinking." She put out fresh mouse poison beneath the sink, something I'd never seen her do. We drove to the hospital and checked her mother out. They were only too glad to see us go. We stuffed her mother into the backseat, which was quite an ordeal. She had to lie down and then we stuffed her legs practically up to her chin. Her mother was screaming and kicking at us. We drove out of town to a wilderness area where I had hiked years ago. We drove in on a little bumpy road until we could hear nothing but the running of a creek. I stopped the car. Roberta

and I looked at each other. Her mother was screaming all the
time. We got out and opened the back door. Her mother kicked
me so hard I stumbled backward and fell. Then she got out of
the car by herself and roared. Rocks tumbled and trees fell.
I crawled to my feet, cowering. Roberta shouted, "Mother, I
love you!" "Hmmpf!" her mother replied. "There is never enough
love." "We'll visit you," Roberta said. "I'll bet you will,"
her mother said, marching off into the darkening hills. "Do
you think she'll be all right?" Roberta said. "She's at the very
top of the food chain. It gets lonely up there," I said.

The Baby

I said, "I'm afraid to go into the woods at night. Please
don't make me go into the woods." "But somebody has stolen our
baby and has taken it into the woods. You must go," she said.
"We don't have a baby, Cynthia. How many times must I tell
you that?" I said. "We don't? I felt certain that we had a
baby," she said. "We will have one soon, I feel certain of
that," I said. "Then it makes no sense for you to go into
the woods at night. Without a baby to search for, what would
you do?" she said. "I'm going to stay right here by the fire
where it's cozy and safe," I said. "I'm going to put the
baby to bed," she said. "Someday there will be a baby," I said.
"Until then I'll put him to bed," she said. "Have it your way,"
I said. She went out of the room humming a little ditty. I
put a log on the fire and lay down on the couch. Cynthia came
running into the room screaming, "The baby is gone! Someone
has stolen our baby!" "I never liked that baby. I'm glad
it's gone. And I'm not going into the woods. Don't even think
of asking me," I said. "A fine father you turned out to be.
My precious baby eaten by wolves," she said.

The Rabbit God

My wife said to me, "Leroy, if you want rabbit stew you're
just going to have to go out there and kill a rabbit." I said,
"I never said anything about wanting rabbit stew." "But you
were acting like you wanted rabbit stew," she said. "I don't
know what you mean by that. I was just being me," I said.
"You were hopping about the living room and, naturally, I took
that to mean you wanted rabbit stew," she said. "I was just
excited by the big game," I said. "I don't know anything about
a big game," she said. "Well, I don't either, but there's always
a big game on. That's the marvel of it," I said. "I still think
you want rabbit stew," she said. "I'm not killing any rabbit,"
I said. "Why? Are you afraid of them?" she said. "No, I'm
too fond of them," I said. "I guess I'm guilty of misreading
the situation. I've always thought I could tell what you were
thinking. Now it seems I have been proven wrong. I have no
idea what you are thinking. It could be anything. You could
be thinking about musk ox or Joe Louis or Kublai Khan or
hoof-and-mouth disease or eustachian tubes or Cheyenne Indians,"
she said. "You're exactly right. I'm thinking about all those
things at once. It makes for a very jumbled experience," I said.
"But I was just making those things up," she said. "So was I,"
I said. "How about rabbit stew?" she said. "Now that's a
smoother road," I said. "Go get your gun," she said. "I don't
have one," I said. "But you had one when we were married,"
she said. "I gave it away," I said. "What kind of man are you?"
she said. "A man without a gun," I said. "Why, you're hardly
a man," she said. "The rabbits think I'm their god. Peaceful
and loving," I said. "Without rabbit stew you are nothing,"
she said.

My Doctor's Appointment

The doctor looked at me and said, "Have you ever stubbed your toe?" "Well, yes, I suppose I have," I said. "That could be the answer right there. Have you ever hummed in public?" he said. "At some point in my life I must have," I said. "There, you see it's coming together. Have you ever thought of the Queen of England naked?" he said. "No, not once, not in all my life," I said. "There's definitely something wrong with you. My guess is that your manganese is off-kilter. Have you ever bitten the head off a chipmunk?" he said. "Maybe once when I was a small child," I said. "Aha, it is coming together now. Have you ever masturbated to a picture of Doris Day?" he said. "Are you crazy?" I said. "I take that to mean you haven't. That's very abnormal for a man of your age. Do you sleep on long train rides?" he said. "I never sleep on trains," I said. "Remind me to check on your pituitary gland. Do you eat watermelon with a knife and fork?" he said. "I would never do that. You'd have to be insane to do that," I said. "Perhaps you are insane. Do elephants ever chase you in a dream?" he said. "Almost every night," I said. "Well, that's good news, at least. Have you ever wanted to throttle a panda?" he said. "I know no pandas," I said. "That's very unusual. Has a UFO ever landed in your backyard?" he said. "Not to my knowledge," I said. "Very interesting. Do you wish one would?" he said. "I have no opinion on the matter," I said. "Most peculiar. Are you tormented by humming-birds?" he said. "I quite like hummingbirds," I said. "That's it. I'm afraid there's nothing I can do for you. You're a hopeless case," he said. "Thank you, Doctor. You're very kind.

This has been very helpful to me. I'll find my way out," I said. He laughed. Halfway down the corridor I was attacked by a mongoose. I tried to shake him, but I couldn't. It was the doctor's own pet.

The Blob

The blob sat there looking at me. Finally, I said, "So
who do you think you are?" It leaned to one side and coughed.
"So why have you come here?" I said. It stared at me and rumbled
in its throat. I was certain it could talk. "Where do you
plan to go when you leave here?" I said. It tried to walk,
but just rolled around on the floor. I was getting angry.
"Why do you behave as if you are an idiot when I know you're not?"
I said. It was drooling now, and its little red eyes popped
in and out of focus. "I hate it when you act like that. I
wish you would talk to me," I said. It stopped wobbling
and seemed to look at me. "Talk to me," I said. "I am an old
weathered bag," it said. "Bag of what?" I said. "How could I know
what's inside? I have never been there," it said. "All right,
let's slow down a bit. What are you looking for?" I said.
"Something to fulfill me," it said. "Yes, and what might that
be?" I said. "How would I know? I'm nearly empty," it said.
"Maybe you long for a mate," I said. "Blurb," it said. "You
want a blurb?" I said. "Blurb blurb," it said. "You are sinking
away from me. I can't understand you," I said. "Blabbykinact,"
it said. "Why are you talking like this? I understood you
perfectly well before," I said. "And you did nothing for me.
Can't you see I'm at an end? It's just so hard for me to speak,"
it said. "Hold on to my hand and I will take you into the future,"
I said. "Bleeblap. I am sinking. Can't you see I am sinking?"
it said. "Grab ahold now," I said. "Zencooyua, farewell,"
it said.

The Psychiatric Unit

I remembered the ashen faces of the children with their
one good arms reaching out to touch their dead mothers and fathers
curled up at their feet. That was the one image that had stuck
in my mind. When I got back to the States they stuck me in
a psychiatric unit with hundreds of other soldiers. We weren't
really supposed to talk about the war, but of course we did.
Sometimes we even cried. Alex asked me if I had even enjoyed
it some days. And I said, "Yes, there were even days when I
thought we were winning." "Yes, I remember those days, but
they were fleeting," he said. Then I took a downturn and they
locked me away. A nurse brought me my food three times a day
and another brought me my medicine twice a day. No one spoke
to me. A doctor finally came. He asked me my name. He asked
me the names of my family members. Then he asked me if I knew
what I was in there for. I said I did not. He said I had failed in
my ability to socialize with the other patients. I said I didn't
know what that meant. He said I was always starting fights and
knocking over tables. I said I didn't remember any of that. He
said how that was often the case. I said I remembered liking
everyone. He said, "Yes, that's very common." He left and I sat
alone in my room. I kept thinking of those little children lying
amidst the dust of their blown-up homes. Where were they now?
I heard a loud scream, and then another. Then all was quiet. There
were bars over the window, so thoughts of escape were not good.
I looked at the white walls. They were shrinking, holding me
tighter and tighter. One day soon they would smother me. And
what can you say about that? That they were doing their job.

Cement

      I had been lifting hundred-pound sacks of cement all day and I was tired, so I lay down on the park bench and tried to sleep. Not five minutes after I closed my eyes a cop poked his nightstick into my ribs and said, "Get up. You can't sleep here. It's against the law." I sat up and said, "What law is that?" "It's called loitering," he said. "I lifted twenty thousand pounds of cement today and you're calling me a loiterer?" I said. "Lying down on the bench is loitering," he said. "I'm guilty, Officer, and if you're not going to arrest me, I will leave the park. Thank you for your leniency. You're a saint," I said. I walked over to the café and ordered a cup of coffee. The waiter said, "You look very tired. Would you like to rent a room upstairs? It's ten dollars an hour." "It's tempting, but I have a home not far from here," I said. "Sometimes there's a pretty woman in the room. You can do with her what you like," he said. "I have a wife who is very good to me," I said. "Sounds like Sunday school," he said. "I just need a cup of coffee," I said. He poured me a cup. A man came in and sat down beside me at the counter. "Nice ferret," I said. "I hate the thing," he said. "Why do you have it?" I said. "I'm taking care of it for a friend," he said. "It's very cute," I said. "It bites me all the time," he said. "Maybe it knows you hate it," I said. "What are you, some kind of ferret psychologist? I don't need this," he said. He got up and moved across the room. I drank my coffee. The ferret bit him on the ear and blood gushed down his neck. He dabbed at it with a paper napkin. I paid for my coffee and left. I walked into an alley and sat down. I closed my eyes. A bum holding a cheap pint of wine walked up to me and said, "It's all rushing away. Can't you feel it?" "What's rushing away?" I said. "Time, it got uncorked. There's no stopping it now. It's like the wind in my hair," he said. "Go to sleep. That will stop it," I said. "It'll be all over soon. There's no time to sleep. It's magnificent, the waves coming and going, the cockatoos in the trees," he said. He took a swig and fell down beside me. He was out cold. I moved his head onto a pile of leaves.

The New Mayor

"Are you just going to stand there and pretend that nothing is happening?" the man said to me. "I don't know what you're talking about," I said. "Well, for one thing the porridge has boiled over and is all over town. The rats and mice are eating it until they explode. It's quite disgusting," he said. "Whose porridge was this?" I said. "Why, it was the king's own porridge," he said. "But we don't have a king," I said. "Don't be daft. Of course we have a king," he said. "If you say so," I said. "Tomorrow morning that cook will be hanged, mark my word," he said. "I've never seen a hanging," I said. "Where've you been? There's at least one a week, sometimes more," he said. "It sounds like we've got a very stern king," I said. "He's a very amusing fellow. I've met him. But he does like to put on a good show. And the crowds love a good hanging," he said. "I don't think I would like to watch one," I said. "Well, you're clearly an odd one," he said. I stopped at a drinking fountain and had myself a drink. He walked on down the street and never looked back. I walked over to the newsstand and bought myself a paper. Then I went over to the park and sat down on a bench. There was a cockatoo up in the tree. Somebody lost their bird. I couldn't take my eyes off of it. It was so beautiful in its aloneness. It took off and landed on top of City Hall, on the clock where it is always the same time. It looked down as if it owned the town, as if it was its mayor. For all I knew maybe it was.

The Photograph of Lincoln

I was driving down this county road. It was just one farm
after another, growing corn, raising cattle. I didn't really
know where I was. The farms had three or four silos and big
barns. Sometimes there were kids playing out front, kickball
and other sports. It was a pretty drive. It could have been fifty
or more years ago. I was trying to find the town of Huntington.
There was an antiques store I'd been meaning to go to for years.
And this was a Sunday where I had nothing to do. Then the road
led me up into the mountains and there were no more farms, just
a little shack every now and then. There were some beautiful
views up there, the river and fields. I stopped to take a picture.
I got back in the car and drove on. There was a sign for Hun-
tington and I felt better. Driving down the mountain I saw a
store. The proprietor asked me where I was from. I told him
and he said, "Never been there." I started looking around. There
was a mounted buffalo head that I liked. There was a very old
pistol from the Civil War. There was a signed photograph of
President Lincoln. There were opera glasses, gowns and tuxedos
from long ago. I wanted everything, but knew I couldn't afford
any of it, so I turned and said good-bye to the owner. He had
fallen asleep at his desk or he was possibly dead. I headed
back the way I had come. On the mountain a man with a rifle
in his hand standing in the middle of the road stopped me. He
came over to my door and said, "My five-year-old son has been
captured by bears, or at least I think he has. I was up on
the mountain hunting with him standing by my side. The next thing
I know he's gone. You've got to help me. When you get down

the mountain go directly to the police and tell them. They're the only chance I've got." I looked behind him. The boy was running down the mountain yelling, "Daddy, Daddy, why did you leave me?"

The

Marcella was filing her nails. She was obviously thinking
about something, but I don't know what it was. I was only her
husband. She shot me a look. "Would you like something, dear?"
I said. "Stop looking at me like that," she said. "Some lemonade?"
I said. "No, I don't want any lemonade," she said. I pretended
to read my book. "Is there something bothering you?" she said.
"No, I'm very much all right. Why do you ask?" I said. "You seem
like you're about to go off on one of your dithering phases,"
she said. "Oh, you know, you wag your head up and down and your
eyes go black, your tongue hangs out," she said. "I don't recall
even remotely ever falling into a state like that," I said. "Well,
you wouldn't. You're completely unconscious," she said. "I'm
just trying to read my book," I said. "That's when it usually
happens," she said. "Oh, Marcella, stop picking on me. I'm
always trying to pick you up. Why do you insist on putting me
down?" I said. "I would never dream of putting you down. All
I was doing was describing some kind of medical condition," she
said. "Let's be nice to one another. What do you say to that?"
I said. "Of course, darling. I wouldn't dream of being other-
wise," she said. I turned back to my book. Marcella was still
filing her nails. "This is a very exciting book," I said.
"You haven't read one word," she said. "Yes, I have.
I read the word 'the,' " I said. "I love the word 'the,' " she said.

My Wife, the Gardener

Marianne was working in the garden. I was washing some dishes and making the bed. I always felt so domestic and peaceful when Marianne worked in the garden. It seemed to slow down time or even stop it. God knows what she was doing out there, pulling weeds, of course, but what else? I could watch her for hours and not know what she was doing. A neighbor's dog came up and sniffed her. She didn't care. I go back to cleaning the house. I mop the bathroom floor. I vacuum the living room rug. I sweep the staircase. I go back to the window. Marianne isn't there. I walk outside and around the house. I still don't see her. I call her name. I look up and down the street. Her car is in the drive-way. Where would she go? I walk over to the garden. Her trowel and spade are there. I pick up the trowel and turn it around in my hand. I start digging up weeds. "Ralph." I see Marianne's hand in the middle of the garden. It's waving to me. I start digging. Pretty soon I have dug her head out. I'm pulling on her arm. Finally I pull her out. "What happened to you?" I say. "I don't know. I was just pulling weeds when something grabbed ahold of me and pulled me down. It was awful. I tried to fight back, but it was too strong. I don't know what it was. It was like the earth wanted to plant me. Like I was a bulb," she said. "You're not a bulb. You're my wife," I said. "Maybe I am a bulb," she said. "You could be a lily," I said. "Yes, I think I am a lily," she said. Then we went inside and fixed lunch.

The Wrong Wedding

There was very little time for small talk, so I said, "Does God exist?" Bruce said, "Who?" I said, "Never mind." He sped around the corner nearly hitting an old lady with her shopping cart. He ran a red light and headed down the hill. He swung left in front of an oncoming car. "Do you believe in life after death?" I said. "Just read me the directions," he said. I read him the directions. "I can't see. The road's all fogged up," he said. "Have you ever seen an angel?" I said. "We've driven off into a pasture. There's a cow," he said. "I love cows. They're so peaceful," I said. "Now what are we going to do? I've lost the damned road," he said. "The fog is lifting. We'll find it," I said. Bruce drove through the field until he finally found his way back onto the road. "We lost some time there. We're going to be late," he said. "I knew a man who lost his leg in the war. He was always late," I said. He swung a right and headed up a steep hill. "This isn't what the directions told us to do," I said. "I know a shortcut," he said. At the top of the hill a moose was standing in the middle of the road. Bruce hit the brakes. He honked the horn. The moose didn't move. He honked it again. Still, nothing. I said, "I'll get out and scare him." "He might kill you," Bruce said. "Moose don't kill people," I said. I got out of the car and took a couple of steps toward him. He let out a tremendous noise that nearly scared me to death. Then he galloped off into the woods. I was still shaking when I got back into the car. "Good work," Bruce said. "That's how you do it," I said. Bruce sped up the rest of the hill and then glided down. "Are you sure you know where we are?" I said. "I'm sure," he said. It was getting dark. After a couple of more turns, he pulled

into the parking lot of a very small church. "Here we are,"
he said. We walked in just as the bride said, "I do." I didn't
recognize anybody. The bride and groom walked down the aisle.
"This is the wrong wedding," I whispered to Bruce. "Oh, they're
all the same," he said.

Assignment Haiti

"I was in Haiti awhile, then they brought me back and I pushed paper around for a couple of years, and now they want to send me back," Wayne said. "And how do you feel about that?" I said. "It's a suicide mission. There's very little chance I will make it back," he said. "And, still, you're going," I said. "It's what I'm trained for. Maybe I can do some good," he said. "You're too young to die," I said. "You're never too young to die in this business," he said. "What if you just say you don't want to go? Can't you quit?" I said. "I pretty much signed up for life. There's no way out unless your health fails you," he said. "I'd rather my health failed me than be dead," I said. "No, I'm going back to Haiti. I might do some good, you never know. I know some of the rebel leaders. They want good things for their country. They're not bad men, but they'll kill you in a second if you get in their way," he said. "Wayne, remember when we were young? There was a cave in back of the house in the woods. How we used to hide in there and wouldn't even come out for dinner, and how we buried our jewels in there and pretended they were worth millions of dollars. We thought pirates were after us and camouflaged our cave with branches," I said. "In what way?" he said. "You're still playing that game, only this time the stakes are for real," I said. "This time they're going to kill me," he said. "And they're going to take your jewels?" I said. "They've already got them," he said.

The Cows

Warplanes were flying over my house on their practice
missions. Nathaniel Mulcahy got drafted, and he was sixty-two
years old. Nobody knows who we are going to attack. They want
it to be a surprise. There are elephants in Borneo. I just
learned that the other day. Nathaniel Mulcahy came over to my
house after he learned he had been drafted. "What am I going
to do? I can't go to war," he said. "There's always Borneo.
You could work in a diamond mine or, if you don't like that,
you could be a fisherman. You could live in a hut," I said.
"I have my farm and eight kids and twenty-three grandkids. I'm
not going anywhere. This is my home," he said. "You could change
your name and have some plastic surgery," I said. "That's not
for me," he said. I got up and started pacing the room. "How
many cows do you have on your farm?" I said. "A hundred and
twenty-three the last I counted," he said. "Did you tell them
that?" I said. "No, I forgot. I was too scared," he said. "See,
you've got to make a case for yourself. We need your milk," I
said. "My cows need me. There's no one else around. All the
kids are grown and moved away," he said. He stood up and put
his hat on. "I just can't picture you dodging bullets," I said.
"My wife shot at me once, but that was long ago. Thanks for
the talk, Chester. Borneo, I'll keep that in mind," he said.
I watched him walk down the driveway. He was an easy target.
He was slow and he limped. He had worked hard all his life.
It would be so easy for me to take him out now.

Toy Soldiers

Scattered about my house are many toy soldiers, but also a few real ones. Sometimes they get me confused. I'd be having a long conversation with one about the nature of the universe and bowling only to realize he was a toy. I'd get so mad I'd throw him across the room and break his head off. Then I'd glue his head back on and be really nice to him. Other times I'd move one from the window ledge to the top of a bookcase and he'd say, "What did you do that for? I like the window ledge." And I'd say, "It doesn't matter what you like. You're mine. I can do with you as I please." "I'm not yours. I am here to protect you, that's all. Now place me back on the window ledge or I will leave you to defend yourself," he said. "Oh, I'm so sorry. I thought you were a toy. If I had known you were a real soldier I would never have touched you," I said. "In a house such as yours filled as it is with many toy soldiers it is understandable that such a mistake might occur every so often, but please note that my weapon is real and I can use it whenever I want. I do not like being set upon a bookcase in the dark," he said. "I'm terribly sorry, and I beg your forgiveness. I do appreciate your protection. I swear I will never again move you, unless of course you ask me to. You are new to me and these others I've had for a very long time. I am always moving them about," I said. "I understand, sir," he said. "It's just that they're all I have," I said. "You are really a very nice man," he said. "Oh, I know, I know, I know," I said. I picked him up and placed him on the windowsill. "That's much better. I can see the flowers in your garden," he said. "They are toy flowers," I said.

The Battlefield

The two ant colonies had declared war on each other and were going at it like crazy, the blacks against the reds. Though the blacks were a little larger than the reds, the killing seemed to be about equal. And both sides were capturing members of the other to spend the rest of their lives as slaves. It was really a brutal battle. It seemed to have been going on all day, perhaps longer. I watched for quite a while, then I had to quit. I walked over to my flower garden to see how it was doing. The irises were in their full bloom. I cut some to take into the house. I went inside and put them in a vase. Then I heard the phone ring. I answered it. It was Ted McCarthy. "How are you doing, Ted?" I said. "I hear you got a real battle going on in your yard," he said. "How'd you know that?" I said. "An ant I know told me about it," he said. "Wait a minute. Ants don't talk," I said. "Yes, they do. You just have to listen very carefully. I taught myself their language," he said. "This is more than I can believe," I said. "You don't have to. I just wanted to know how the battle was going," he said. "It looked like it was a draw the last I looked," I said. "My informant said the reds had lots of reserves," he said. "I don't know about that," I said. "He said the reds would crush them in the end," he said. "Well, it was certainly a vicious fight the last I saw," I said. "Do you want to bet on the outcome?" he said. "No, that's not the kind of thing I would bet on," I said. "Just ten dollars," he said. "No, I'm not going to bet on it," I said. He hung up on me. It wasn't fair. He had a spy.

Peace

I sat on the porch watching the sunset. It was especially beautiful tonight, seeming to last a long time. A flock of ducks flew over hurrying toward their pond. I felt very peaceful. My job was going well. I had been given a raise. I was next in line for manager. The sun was down and the lightning bugs had come out. There was a full moon in the sky. A man walked out onto the porch. "Who are you?" I said. "I'm your double agent, but you can call me Chad," he said. "And how did you get in here?" I said. "I picked your lock. We're very good at things like that," he said. "But I don't understand what you want," I said. "I'm just going to follow you around, see how you live," he said. "But why would you want to do that?" I said. "It's my job. I was assigned to you," he said. "But what's the point of it? I'm just your average Joe," I said. "We need more information on your average Joe, as you say," he said. "I don't think I like this. I'm going to call the police. They could arrest you for breaking and entering," I said. "The police are our friends. We cooperate with them all the time," he said. "I could shoot you," I said. "Don't be silly. I would shoot you before you got the gun," he said. "Well, then, we might as well be friends. Can I get you a beer?" I said. "I'm not allowed to drink on the job, but thanks for the offer. Mind if I sit down?" he said. "Of course not, make yourself comfortable," I said. "You were just sitting here by yourself doing nothing?" he said. "I watched the sunset. It was quite lovely," I said. "Isn't that against the law?" he said. "Not that I know of," I said. "Well, you're an absurd man," he said. "Maybe I am, maybe I'm not. It makes no difference to me. Now get out of

this house before I tear your head off," I said. I chased him out
of the front door, pounding on his head. I went back to the
front porch and gazed at the stars. There is so much trouble
in the world a little peace is a precious thing.

The Oilman

Owen said, "Do you know where I can get a gun?" "Well,
there are lots of places to get a gun, but what would you want
a gun for?" I said. "See that man over there? He's been following
me for days," he said. "Let's go talk to him, see what he wants,"
I said. "Oh, no, that's not allowed. You can't just walk up
to the man that's following you and ask him that," he said. "It
seems like the only sensible thing to do if you ask me," I said.
"It's bad manners. Gangsters have their rules, you know," he said.
"Well, I'm going, if you don't care to join me, that's fine," I
said. The man had on sunglasses and a fedora. I walked up to
him and said, "Are you following that guy over there?" "Yeah,
what of it?" he said. "I was just curious," I said. "Don't
spoil my cover," he said. "I won't, promise," I said. I walked
back to Owen. "What'd he say?" Owen said. "He's following you,"
I said. "I'm going to go get a gun," he said. "Maybe he just likes
you," I said. "Look at that guy. He doesn't look like anybody," he
said. "He seemed like a real nice fellow to me," I said. We
took off walking. We walked to the park where mothers were pushing
their kids on swings. I looked around. He was standing behind
a tree. I could see the hem of his overcoat hanging out. I said
to Owen, "Let's sneak up on him and jump him." Owen said, "You
don't do things that way. That would be considered very rude."
"But what if he's going to kill you?" I said. "I haven't got that
far yet," he said. "Maybe you do need a gun," I said. "It's too
late for that," he said. The man behind the tree stepped out.
He stood there for a moment, then walked toward us. "You have
neglected to pay your oil bill. It is a week overdue," he said.
"But I meant to pay it. I don't know what happened," Owen said.

"Good intentions don't count. Have the check in our office this afternoon or else," he said. "You'll have it, I promise," Owen said. The man looked at me and lifted his sunglasses. "You have poor taste in company," he said. He left the park and disappeared into the crowd. "He could have killed you," I said. "I know," Owen said.

After the War

The Queen of England had written me a note saying how
grateful she was for all I had done for her. I tried hard to
remember exactly what it was I had done for her. I could think
of nothing. Then I remembered the war. I had rescued a maiden
from a burning farmhouse. And, later, we had fallen in love.
I had gone back to my duty in the trenches, but every day I
thought of her. And then when I was wounded her letters pulled
me through. There is no question I would have died without them.
And when the war was over I went looking for her. No one had
ever heard of her, my little Jenny. I asked everyone I met.
I went to her old house, which had been repaired, and no one there
recognized her name or picture. I was falling into despair.
Finally, I returned home, a broken man. It took me months to
pull myself together. I started working for a lumber company.
It was not very exciting at first, but still I worked hard.
The manager liked me, because we were both veterans. He gave
me more and more responsibility. One night I met a woman at a
company square dance. I could tell she liked me, so I kept asking
her to dance. A year later we were married. All she wanted to
do was have babies. We had four in our first five years of marriage.
By that time I was tired of her. The kids drove me nuts. I loved
them, but there was no peace in the house. I thought of running
away, I thought of it constantly. But then the kids got older
and things started to settle down a bit. Heather and I fell back
in love. We were planning a second honeymoon, when this letter
from the Queen of England arrived and I realized she was Jenny.
Heather and I went to the Bahamas, while the Queen sat on her
little potty and cried. Isn't that how it's supposed to end?

Conspiracy

I said, "Well, I certainly don't know anything about any
of this." Mr. Black said, "Well, you've certainly landed in
the middle of it." I said, "I don't even know what it is."
"It's a conspiracy of like-minded souls to undermine the govern-
ment," he said. "Why would I care to be a part of something
like that?" I said. "You would like to bring down our govern-
ment," he said. "I don't think about our government one way
or another," I said. "Of course you do. Everybody thinks about
our government one way or another," he said. "But I don't. I
am completely oblivious to our government," I said. "That's
not possible. You pay your taxes, don't you? You follow certain
laws. The government is always telling you what to do," he said.
"Yes, but I try to ignore it. I just do things my own way,"
I said. "And your way happens to coincide with what the govern-
ment is telling you to do?" he said. "I've never really thought
about it, I guess so," I said. "I don't believe you. You are
out to tear the whole thing down. I know your type," he said.
"I am not, I assure you. I don't care one bit about the govern-
ment," I said. "See, that's what I mean. Only somebody like
yourself could have made these plans," he said. "I'm not like
anybody you have met before. I don't care what you say. You're
not going to twist me into this thing," I said. "You are already
there. Everything you say points to your guilt," he said.
"Then I'll not say anything more," I said. We sat there in our
chairs for a long time until he finally fell asleep. Crickets
were chirruping outside. I thought about the keys on his belt,
then fell into my own deep sleep, where antelope jumped the fence
each night and were caught captive by the farmer in the mornings.

The Soldiers' Rebellion

Slow lobbing balls of light were being fired at me. Then I realized I was surrounded. Little toy soldiers were firing at me. They were mine, but I had not placed them there. I was hiding behind the sofa. There was no way out. I called to the men to stop firing. They didn't listen. Cannons fired, machine guns burst. Of course it was all in the realm of toys, but still it was frightening. I crawled over to a wastebasket and threw it in the air. You could hear the bullets pinging off of it like crazy. I tried to peek my head up, but the bullets went zinging past so fast I had to hit the ground. I could hear men inching up on me on both sides of the couch. Suddenly I jumped up and screamed. All was silent for a moment. Then shots started firing again. I jumped over the couch and ran into the bedroom. I locked the door. My wife said, "What's wrong with you?" "Oh, nothing. You know how things go. I touch the wrong button on the oven and everything goes crazy," I said. "Well, you should go back out there and confront it," she said. "Yes, I know, this is no way to behave. This is really cowardly of me," I said. "You're the boss, George. You can fix it," she said. "I'm going right now," I said. I went to the closet and got a hat and some goggles. "George, what's wrong with you?" she said. "You never know what might happen," I said. One of the soldiers had slipped under the door. He shot me in the ankle. "Ouch!" I said. "What's wrong with you, George?" she said. "I've been shot in the ankle," I said. He shot me again in the arm. "Ouch!" I said. "Are you okay?" she said. "I'm definitely not okay. I'm wounded," I said. "What's going on in here?" she said. "My little men have risen up and they're not going to take it anymore," I said. "Take what?" she said. "I don't know," I said.

The Captain

"We're not going into battle as we had planned, because the captain has a stomachache," the sergeant said to me. "Well, then, maybe I'll go home and see my wife," I said. "I don't think that would be a good idea, because the captain wants to talk to everyone at dinner, that is, if he's well enough," he said. "He puts the whole war on hold because of an upset stomach, then he won't let us see our wives, he's crazy," I said. "That's the way it is," he said. "Well, I don't like it," I said. He walked away and I sat on my bunk in the barracks. Perkins walked up to me. "We could just go to war without him," he said. "He gives the orders, but nobody ever follows him," I said. "I know I never have," he said. "I've always disagreed with him," I said. "Do you know who the enemy is?" he said. "Not really," I said. "Do you know how we could find out?" he said. "He keeps it secret from us until the last minute so it'll be a surprise," I said. "Maybe I could steal his playbook," he said. "He'd kill you if he caught you," I said. "I'll watch him and take it when he's in the bathroom," he said. "You're crazy," I said. "Then we wouldn't need him," he said. "It doesn't hurt to wait one day," I said. "But don't you see the beauty of my plan?" he said. "It's just too dangerous," I said. "You're a coward is what you are," he said. I punched him in the face and then one in the stomach. He lay there on the floor groaning. "The captain's sick, show some respect. He may be a poor captain, but he's all we have," I said.

The Escape

      I lay in the dark and waited. The guard came along and kicked me in the ribs. "Oh," I said. He was looking for the dead ones. He went on kicking the captives. One of them said, "I want to see my representative." He gave him a couple of extra kicks. And so it went through the night. One could sleep between the visits from the guards, but that was all. Then the bells went off at six o'clock. We had a brief breakfast, and then we went to work in the trenches. We dug all day with a twenty-minute break for lunch. If we slacked off at all we were beaten with a whip. I kept sneaking glances around the camp. I told Frank one night, "I'm going to escape. Do you want to come, too?" He said, "It's impossible. There are guards everywhere." "We'll find a way," I said. We kept working every day. One of our men was beaten to death for picking his nose. I said, "That's it. I've had it." I told Frank it was the next night. When night fell, we attacked one of the guards and gagged and bound him. Then we crawled outside the tent and hid in the tall grass. We attacked another guard and left him unconscious. It was a night without moonlight. Frank said, "What are we going to do?" I said, "I know a way into the mountains." When another guard passed, we took off running. We ran without interference. I said, "I think I'm going to drop." He said, "Let's stop here." There were huge waves in front of us. He said, "I thought you said there were mountains?" "I was wrong. It must be the ocean," I said. "What are we going to do with the ocean?" he said. "Just walk along the beach. No one goes here anymore," I said. Just then a bunch of young girls in bikinis came running toward us. "What are those?" he said. "I don't know. Must be something from another planet," I said.

Night-Wandering Animal

The more I thought about it the more I didn't want to go to that meeting. They were nothing but a bunch of bitter, old people who had nothing better to do than plan for the town's eventual destruction. I thought they were just amusing.
I played along at first, joking, making wry comments. But after a while I saw they were moving toward a real plan. It ceased to be funny, and I felt I was caught in a nightmare. I told Buddy and he laughed it off. Then they blew up the State House. The police didn't know who they were after, but, still, we lay low, pretended we didn't exist. That's when I started thinking of getting out. I didn't answer my messages for a while. If I saw one of them on the street we barely spoke. Then I heard that the police had a trace on the men who had committed the crime. Next I know they had picked them up. I really wanted out of the group. I despised them all, except Buddy. I saw the ruins of City Hall and it made me want to cry. I called Buddy and told him I was thinking about leaving town. He said, "Don't leave. If they look for you and can't find you, they'll assume you're guilty." "But this is too much for me. I feel like I'm ready to explode," I said. "Calm down. You didn't do anything," he said. "I know, but we were part of the group, and they planned it," I said. "You didn't know it was being planned. They never said anything in front of us, did they?" he said. "No, but we were always there at the meetings," I said. Someone was knocking at my door. I said a quick good-bye to Buddy and went and peeked out the window. It was the police. I grabbed my coat and knife and went to the bedroom window. I opened it and crawled out and ran for the woods as fast as I could. I was never going back. There was nowhere else to go.

Explosive Device

I said to Jody, "Well, what do you think is going to happen to us?" "They're going to capture us and shoot us," she said. "No, really, let's not be so dramatic. What do you really think?" I said. "How would I know? Surely the government would like to punish us. They have to set an example," she said. "But what have we really done? We haven't been accused of anything. They can't just pick us out of a crowd and say I don't like the way you look," I said. "They can do whatever they want. Just give them a chance," she said. "All right, so I'm guilty of bad thoughts. That's not punishable by law, is it?" I said. "If they can prove you intended to act on those thoughts, it is," she said. "Who's to say what I might have done? I have changed my mind many times," I said. "Yes, but you had the thought, that's what matters," she said. "I've had a million thoughts, which one really counts?" I said. "The one they can prove you guilty of," she said. "Who's going to tell them what that is? They can't read my mind," I said. "The last we knew they couldn't. Maybe things have changed," she said. "Well, then, we're all going to hell," I said. "Yes, perhaps, we are," she said. "You don't really think like that and neither do I. We're just being a little paranoid," I said. The sun was just setting. "Let's go out on the porch and watch the sun set. I like to listen to all the birds," I said. "Those birds are prerecorded and played back to us," she said. "No, they're not," I said. "Yes, they are," she said. "I don't believe you," I said. "You don't know what you're talking about," she said. "I do too," I said. "No, you don't," she said. And so the evening passed. Some kind of small explosive device was ticking in her mind where there had been none before.

The Invasion

I was standing outside the dress shop waiting for somebody.
Well, I wasn't really waiting for somebody, I was pretending to
wait for somebody. I had come to town, but then I forgot what
it was I wanted. Maybe I never wanted anything. I just needed
the company. Then Lottie walked out of the shop. I said, "Hello,
Lottie, I was just waiting for you." She said, "That's nice,
but why would you wait for me?" "No reason, really, I just
thought we could spend a few minutes together," I said. "Well,
okay, what would you like to talk about?" she said. "I thought
maybe you could recite to me a few lines by Longfellow," I said.
"I don't know anything by Longfellow," she said. "Perhaps Vachel
Lindsay," I said. "I'm sorry, no Vachel Lindsay, either," she said.
"I'm sorry, I really just ran into you by mistake. I didn't know
you were in there," I said. "That's what I figured. Where are
you going?" she said. "I was on my way to the invasion," I said.
"What invasion? What are you talking about?" she said. "The
French troops are set to invade the town. They're just outside
of it now," I said. "Oh my God, what am I going to do?" she said.
"You must take cover or get outside of town as fast as you can,"
I said. "But I loaned my car to my sister. What am I going to do?"
she said. "I know a hidden cave we can go to. It's not too far
from here," I said. So we took off running from the middle of town,
me helping Lottie with her packages, Lottie tripping and nearly
falling. When we got there Lottie paused and looked at it. "It's
just a little hole in the earth," she said. "Go inside and see
for yourself," I said. She knelt and started to crawl in. "Wow!
It's beautiful," she said. I crawled in behind her. I hadn't
been in there since I was a kid. "There are even cave paintings

on the wall," she said. I had made those as a kid, but I didn't tell her. We stayed there until nightfall, cuddled in the dark. We heard no gunshots or wailing. Lottie said, "I don't think anything happened." "I guess not," I said. "You were fooling me all along, weren't you?" she said. "You can't be too cautious," I said. "Thank you. I enjoyed that," she said.

The Mission

This equipment onshore looked like it needed repair, so we walked back to the cabin to talk it over. Frank said he was going home tomorrow and I said, "You can't go home. You have to stay here with me and we'll get it fixed and take it in the boat to the other side of the lake." He said, "I can't do that, I have other things waiting for me back home." "You said you would do this for me. That other stuff can wait," I said. He went to bed and when he got up in the morning he started to pack. I said, "Frank, you know without us they're going to lose. Did you think about that?" "I don't care anymore. Both sides are losers to me," he said. "But, Frank, think of your family. Do you really want them to live under the power of the bad guys?" I said. "They're all bad guys. Can't you see, there's no difference," he said. And so I stayed on in the cabin by myself. I went down to the beach and studied the equipment. I tried to fix it by myself. I got the motor to run. I decided that was good enough. I found someone to help me launch the boat. I was out there on the waters by myself. I realized Frank had the map, how that happened I'll never know. I was steering blindly. Where would I go if I were a rebel force? Hell, it all looked good to me. I picked a direction and stayed with it. After about three hours I was nearing the shore. I threw down the anchor and prepared to disembark. "Alex! Alex!" I cried. Alex was the name of our captain. No one replied. I climbed up onto the beach and looked around. A bonfire was still smoldering. Some children ran out onto the beach and leapt into the water. I yelled after them, "Hey, who are you?" One of them yelled back, "We're the children of paradise, who do you think we are?" "Have you seen the rebel forces?" I said. "They left days ago," he said. Somebody had told me that this was a necessary mission. Now I felt quite foolish. I stood there on the beach watching the kids bob and dive about in the water. I knew not where I was.

Investigation

After the war you couldn't get a pint of blood anywhere.
You couldn't even buy a pair of socks. I went into a restaurant
and ordered a steak and they nearly ran me out. I called the
appliance company and told them my air conditioner was broken
and they started laughing. It seemed we were out of everything.
It wasn't just luxury items either. So I locked up my house
and headed for the woods. I figured I could find everything
I needed out there. There was a place near Green Mountain
where I had camped before. When I got there all there was for
as far as the eye could see was charred ground, nothing living
anywhere. There must have been a fire or something. I looked
at the map. I was only an hour from the coast, so I took off
driving. When I got there it was empty. I went to a small
hotel and checked in. The clerk looked so happy to see me. I
asked the clerk where was everybody. He said all the customers
disappeared about a week ago. He didn't know where they went.
I went to my room. The bed wasn't made, the trash wasn't
emptied. Still, I made myself comfortable and looked out
at the sea. After a while I called the desk. I said, "This is
Room 32. I have a kind of funny question for you. We did win
the war, didn't we?" "That's what I've been told," he said.
"Yes, well, thank you. I was just wondering," I said. I went
back to looking at the sea. There were no boats anywhere. I
tried to imagine what the fishermen were doing. After a while
I left the room and went downstairs. The clerk waved me over
and said to me, "I heard they've all been rounded up." "The

enemy?" I said. "No, our side," he said. "What for?" I said. "Investigations," he said. "Investigating what?" I said. "Somebody threw a mud ball at the president's childhood girl-friend," he said. "Oh," I said.

The Wrong Man

The police were as thick as flies down there. Perhaps
they'd caught the bomber, I don't know. I stayed in the house
and lowered the blinds. Then I made myself some eggs for lunch.
I finished and then cleaned up. There was a knock on the door.
I opened it and it was a Boy Scout. "What do you want?" I said.
"Would you like to buy some cookies?" he said. "Go away," I said.
"What?" he said. "How much are they?" I said. "They're three
dollars a pack," he said. "I'll take ten," I said. "That's very
good," he said. "Here's the thirty dollars, now I think you should
go," I said. "Here's your receipt," he said. I slammed the door
in his face. I locked the door and hid under the bed. Maybe
an hour passed that way. Then I slowly climbed from under the
bed and brushed myself off. I was covered in dust babies. In one
hand I was holding an African spear. I don't remember ever
seeing that before. I set it down on the bed and brushed myself
off. I went and peeked out the window. They were all gone.
I went around the house opening the blinds. In the backyard a fox
was eating some mulberries. I went out on the front porch and
sat in the swing. My neighbor, who was raking his lawn, looked
up and waved to me. I waved back and said what a nice day it was.
He said, "It sure is. Did you hear, they caught the bomber right
down the street." "That's good news," I said. Then he went back
to raking. The next thing I know the house next door blew
up and I thought, they caught the wrong man.

The Grandson

I never saw even a picture of my grandson until it was
too late. He was born in Odessa and moved to Moscow when
he was two. His father worked for the state and his mother
was an artist. I lived in a small town north of Leningrad
and was a shoemaker. After my daughter's son was born her
work caught fire, earning her a hot reputation both here and
abroad. She couldn't turn out canvases fast enough. My son-
in-law was proud of her but a little ashamed at his offices.
Then one day she disappeared. The husband looked all over
for her. He just couldn't believe it. In this day and age.
They took my grandson too. What harm could he do? The husband
felt so alone in the world. Of course he suspected his
colleagues at work knew something of the matter, at least a few
of them. I went down to stay with him, finally. The place
was a mess, and he was too. I suggested we put my daughter
and her son's things in boxes, but he wouldn't hear of it.
We made maps of where she traveled most days, then divided
the territories up for us to visit. I went to a café in the
morning. She had had coffee there the morning of her dis-
appearance. I followed down my list: library, bookstore,
paint store. Everyone had seen her that day, nothing out of
the ordinary. I stayed several weeks. No clues turned up.
I went back home. Then a month later I got a letter from
Sergei that said, "They're back! She says they were off to
America on a spying mission, but I know better. She had a
tryst with an art critic named Malofsky in Syracuse. I forgive
her, because life with me must be terribly boring. She
hasn't mentioned the baby. I think he'll show up in time."

Life's Game

We heard no one coming, so we snuck out of our house on our hands and knees. We crawled around the corner down by the firehouse. We heard three shots fired. Then a long silence. I said to Denea, "Let's stand up." We stood up. She said, "Let's write 'help' on the side of the firehouse." "What'll we write it with?" I said. "My lipstick," she said. "Good idea," I said. So she wrote HELP with her lipstick. "Anybody who sees that will probably be dead," I said. "I didn't think of that," she said. "Let's get out of here," I said. So we ran around in back and down the hill. We hid behind some trees and caught our breath. Two more shots were fired. One of them nicked the tree behind which I stood. I looked at Denea. "Let's make a run for that wall," I said, pointing to the toy store. The toy store had been closed a long time, a year or so. When we got there we rested and looked around. We didn't see anyone. But then part of the toy store blew up and the other half fell down on its own. We were completely exposed. "Let's get out of here," she yelled, and we took off running down the street. A hand grenade went off in front of us and we dove and rolled in the grass. "Hey, wait a minute, this is beginning to seem very much like the video game I played yesterday. I recognize everything about it, the bombs, the bullets, the hand grenade. We're playing a 3-D version of that game, I swear it," I said. "I don't believe you. It can't be true," she said. "Watch this," I said. I waved my hand above me and shots were fired. I stood up and a bullet hit me right between the eyes. "I'm dead," I said. "Oh my God, you're right," she said.

The Guards

A soldier marched up and down our street every morning
for nearly an hour. One morning I went out and asked him why
he was doing it. "To protect you from the enemy," he said.
"Who's the enemy?" I said. "This I have not been informed
about," he said. "Well, I hope you get him," I said. "Yes,
sir," he said. I went back in the house and made myself a
cup of coffee. My wife came downstairs and stared out the
window. "Should we invite him in?" she said. "I don't think
so. He has important work to do," I said. "Yes, of course,"
she said. One morning we were leaving the house for work and
we found the soldier dead in our rose garden. We panicked.
We didn't know what to do. "Call the police," I said. "Yes,
of course," she said. The next day there was a new soldier
in front of our house. We made friends with him, brought him
sandwiches for lunch. Then one day we returned from work and
he lay dead in our front yard. "What are we going to do?"
my wife said. "Well, we're going to call the police and then
we'll request that they not send us any more soldiers," I said.
Several weeks went by without guards. Even though they got
killed we missed them. One night we were watching television
when a bullet shot through our living room window, shattering
it. We both screamed and dove for the rug. A moment later
there was a knock on the door. I crawled to the door and
answered it. An officer stood there and said, "Just making sure
you were all right." "Oh, yes, Officer," I said, "things have
never been better," wiping the glass from my pants.

The Lost Army

From where I stood the troops appeared very small. Then
they came closer and they still seemed quite diminutive. That's
when I realized I was looking through the wrong end of my binoculars.
I was so embarrassed I threw them away. Now the troops appeared
quite close and of normal stature. I jumped out of the bushes
and yelled, "Surprise!" The soldiers in the front immediately
took aim, but their captain said to halt. I said, "Hi, my name
is Jaime and I'll be your guide." The soldiers all looked to
their captain and he shrugged his shoulders. "Well, come on, boys,
let's march," I said. And I started marching. First, we marched
over the hill, between oaks and maples and weeping willows. Then
down the hill, between burned-out Chevrolets and Fords. Then
along a long plain populated by Burger Kings and Kentucky Fried
Chickens. "Where would you like to stop for lunch?" I asked the
captain. "McDonald's would be my choice," he said. We found one
right away and ate there. Afterwards he suggested we all take
a nap. It made sense to me. So we slept for forty-five minutes outside
under some fake palm trees. The captain said, "Fall in." And all
the soldiers obeyed. I stood beside the captain, and he whispered
to me, "Where now?" "Straight ahead, sir," I said. We marched
through a park where lots of kids were playing. Then through a shop-
ping center with lots of traffic. I said to the captain, "I need
to stop here to buy some underwear. Would you wait?" "A few
minutes," he said. I went inside, started shopping around. One
stop led to another, and pretty soon I was doing my Christmas
shopping. I forgot all about the army. When I left the mall they
were gone. I found a stray one now and then in my wanderings, but
nothing I could call an army.

The Key to the Universe

       I saw a sleigh being pulled by horses and filled with
laughing and cheering people disappear down the hill. I
immediately began to wonder if I had imagined it. I put on
my boots and coat and walked out the door and over to the hill.
There were the tracks, all right, and the horses' footsteps.
The voices still faintly hung in the air. I was relieved.
I started to walk back home. A man in a balloon passed over
and shouted to me, "I'm going to crash. Please help me!" I
tried to see where he was going. I ran back home and got in
my car. The balloon was sinking just below the horizon and
I took after it. There was an open field in back of the Doubledays'
house and I figured he was trying to land there. When I arrived
he wasn't there. There was a man walking a dog on the street.
I went up to him and said, "Did you see a balloon go over here?"
"No. I saw three crows, though," he said. "I'm talking about
a balloon with a man in it," I said. "If I'd seen a thing like
that I'd surely remember," he said. I drove around a little,
then gave up and went back home. There was a little man standing
on my back steps. "I have something for you," he said. "What
is it?" I said. "You have to guess," he said. "I'm not going
to guess," I said. "I'll give you three guesses," he said. "It
could be anything in the world. How am I going to guess?" I
said. "Come on, guess," he said. "I'm not going to guess," I
said. "Come on, play along with me," he said. "An apple," I
said. "No, come on, you got two more," he said. "A diamond
ring," I said. "No, come on, think hard, what is it I have for
you?" he said. "I don't know," I said. "Yes, you do know, think
hard," he said. "The key to the universe," I said. "That's

exactly right. I knew you could do it. You have the key to the universe," he said. "It sounds very impressive, but what's it for?" I said. "I'm not sure. Let me read the instructions," he said, putting on his glasses. It was just a little piece of paper, but he read it for quite a long time. "What's it say?" I said finally. "It says, 'Don't forget the pancake mix,'" he said. "What else?" I said. "It says, 'Call Charlie,'" he said.

The Pandas of Wichita

"Does anybody know where the spare panda parts are?" Denice asked. "I believe they were shipped to Siberia," Bruce said. "They were supposed to go to Wichita," Wayne said. "Well, there's an expiration date on them," Denice said. "It's not my fault," Bruce said. "I can place a phone call," Wayne said. "Do you have any idea what they were worth?" Denice said. "I'd rather not think about it," Bruce said. "They'll have our heads for this one," Wayne said. "That's for sure," Denice said. "We might as well shoot one another," Bruce said. "Why don't we claim we never saw them? Throw the blame on somebody else," Wayne said. "They're not idiots. Their records are complete. They know every stop along the way," Denice said. "I want to get the hell out of here before they find out. I don't know about the rest of you," Bruce said. "They'll just hunt us down, and you know what will happen then," Wayne said. "What if I reported that we'd been robbed?" Denice said. "No one would believe you. There are alarms that would have been set off," Bruce said. "They are going to have our heads one way or another," Wayne said. "Is there any way to replace the panda parts?" Denice said. "They are among the rarest commodities on the planet," Bruce said. "Did either of you notice that we keep speaking in this same exact order? First Denice speaks, then Bruce, then me. It's as though we are trained monkeys," he said. "Monkeys can't speak," Denice said. "Monkeys couldn't possibly do what we do," Bruce said. "I like monkeys," Wayne said. "I was wondering if we could fashion the panda parts out of some old rubber tubing," Denice said. "I've got some baboon livers," Bruce said. "Now we're talking. I've got some pipe cleaners," Wayne said. "The pandas of Wichita glub, snort, tinkle, fall. The end," said Denice.

Depression

One day in summer I was walking through town looking in
the store windows. I looked in the back of one and saw Wendy
trying on a new dress. "You look great, Wendy," I yelled.
She looked and squinted and said, "Oh, thanks, Keith. I think
I'll get it," she said. I walked on. Down by the post office
I ran into Mark. "Can I talk to you a second?" he said. "Well,
sure, Mark," I said. "Have you seen Angie?" he said. "No, I
haven't," I said. "Well, she looks awful. She hasn't bathed in
a week. She's depressed. She's about to lose her job. Plus,
she suddenly can't stand me. I don't think she likes anybody
really," he said. "Sounds like depression. My sister had it
once. She also wouldn't bathe and turned on all those close
to her," I said. "What did you do?" he said. "We got her to
go to a doctor. He gave her some medicine and she got better,"
I said. "Do you remember the doctor's name?" he said. "No, but
my mother might. She takes all kinds of pills. She must get
them from somewhere," I said. "Well, if she'll tell you, give
me a call," he said. We said our good-byes and parted. My mother
had every kind of pill under the sun. She'd call me late at
night and I couldn't understand her. I went on to the other
stores, the gift shop, the used book store, the toy shop. I went
in the toy shop. I drifted over to the table where they had all
the little rubber animals. Anything you wanted for only a dollar
apiece. I selected a yak, an alligator, and a lamb. I paid
for them up front. Then I went to the cemetery in back of the
store. I found my mother's grave and placed them on it. She
never did like flowers. Too much trouble.

The American Dream

Alan Ross came to me one day and said he wanted
to escape the rat race. I said, "What are you going to do?"
He said, "I don't know. I'm thinking about it." "It's not so
easy to escape, you know. You have to have money." He said,
"I know. I don't have any." "Well, you have a little problem,
don't you?" I said. "I'll think of something, I will," he said.
That was the last time I saw Alan. A month went by. I thought
about Alan all the time. I couldn't imagine where he'd gone.
I said to Liliann, "How could he get by without any money?" She
said, "People can live by their charm. They do it all the time."
"Alan isn't charming," I said. "He could be if he needed to be,"
she said. After a couple of more months I forgot him. I worked
hard at my job and got a raise. Liliann and I took a vacation
into the mountains. I fished and she read her books. It was so
relaxing I almost forgot I worked. But then it was over and I
went back to work. Something went wrong one day and I caused us
to lose a fortune. My boss said, "Get out. I don't ever want to
see you again." I said, "I can make it up, I'm certain." He said,
"Get out, you're fired." I didn't want to go home. I didn't know
where to go. I sat on the steps of the bank with my head in my
hands. A man came along and said, "I can help you. I know a
place for people like you." I said, "I don't think so. I'm
a ruined man. There is no place for someone like me." "Yes, there
is. You must follow me," he said. And so I got up and followed
him. We got on a bus and took it to the end of the line. "Where
are we going?" I asked him. "It's just a short walk," he said.
We walked several miles. I was dead tired. There was Alan, all
skin and bones. I said, "Alan, what are you doing here?" He said,
"I don't know. I'm just a slave. They said it was for the
American dream," he said. "But what kind of dream is that?" I
said. "It's like something you wish you'd never known," he said.

Home

There were no stars in the sky when I set off on my trek.
It was just me and my backpack. There was a slight chill in the
air. I walked fast at first, but after a few hours I slowed
down. My goal was to reach Lake Waumaconga and rest for a few
hours. Once I saw the lake I collapsed on its shores. I
didn't know how tired I was. I slept for a few hours and when
I awoke there were two moose bathing in the waters. I didn't
want to disturb them, so I just lay there and watched them.
Eventually they left and I got up and stretched. Then it was on
to Milbrook, some thirty miles from there. I hiked through the
countryside, spotting several eagles on the way. One farmer came
at me with a shotgun and told me to get off his land. I apologized
and left his farm as quickly as I could. At a café where I had
stopped for coffee the waitress seemed to like me. I told her
and she said her grandmother was from there. "We're almost
cousins," I said. "Almost," she said and went to wait on others.
When I finished my coffee I left her a good tip and said good-bye
on my way out. I picked up the trail again which headed into
the mountains. They were more like large, rounded hills than
mountains. When I reached the top of the first one I noticed
all these weird, little cairns about. Obviously there had been
quite a bit of human traffic there, young folks. I was tempted
to rest again, but I kept going, down the other side. I stumbled
and fell several times. The rocks kept sliding beneath my feet.
Then I fell in a hole. I kept falling. Then when I landed I
heard voices all around me. "He's here." "I knew he'd come."
"Thank God, he's here at last." "What are we going to do with

him?" "Where am I?" I said. "You're home," several of them said. "Where's that?" I said. After a brief silence, one of them said, "Why don't you ask us where your belly button is?" And they all broke into hysterical laughter. "Where's my belly button?" I said.

Greatness

The old man dropped dead in the middle of the street. I was standing nearby and ran up to him. I tried giving him artificial respiration, but it did no good. An ambulance arrived and they took him away. I stood there with some others until they finally drifted away. Then I went and got a cup of coffee at the local diner. I tried to read the paper, but my mind drifted back to the dead man. Who was he? Did he have a wife? Children? I wondered how old he was. Was he in the war? Of course none of this mattered anymore. He was dead. I finished my coffee and left the café. I went to the pharmacy and got a prescription filled. Then I went to the men's store and bought a pair of socks. When I got home I thought about dinner. Was there anything to eat in the house? Some macaroni and carrots? I went and sat on the porch. I watched Mr. Patterson mow his lawn. He must have been eighty years old, but, still, he managed. He had been in the Marines sixty years ago. A butterfly flew by, then landed on a rosebush. I went inside, had dinner, read a book, and went to bed. When I woke up in the morning, I got the paper. There was an obituary for the dead man I saw on the street. He had been an Olympic athlete in his youth, had won a gold medal in track. Then things started to go downhill for him. He got a job as a high school gym teacher and within a couple of years he fell in love with a fourteen-year-old gymnast. He was fired from the job, but he went on to marry the girl. An arrest warrant was put out nationwide and they lived hand to mouth for the next four years, always just a step ahead of the law. When the law stopped chasing him, he got a job as a dishwasher in a little café. He washed dishes, then he cooked, then managed, and finally, after twenty-five years, owned the place he called Champ's. After ten years of relative success his wife died. He lost interest in the place and just walked the streets. He died a year later. And to think I had put my mouth to his. I had touched greatness!

An Eel on the Line

I tried to call Iceland. I asked for Hans Magnus Chris-
tenson. The operator said there are forty-seven men by that
name. I said, "Well, this one has only one leg." She said,
"There are three men with only one leg. Which leg does he have?"
I said, "He has only his right leg." She said, "There are two
men with only their right leg." I said, "What are their ages?"
She said, "One is eighty-seven and the other is thirty-two."
I said, "Could you give me the number of the one who is eighty-
seven?" She gave it to me. "Thank you very much," I said.
I dialed the number. "Hello," he said. "Hello, Grandpa," I
said. "What?" he said. "I said, 'Hello, Grandpa.'" "I can't
hear you," he said. "I said, 'Hello, Grandpa.'" "There's an
eel on the line," he said. "An eel?" I said. "Yes, I would
like some eel," he said. "I'll be sure to send you some," I
said. "Some what?" he said. "Some eel," I said. "Yes, I believe
we have some eel on our line," he said. "Are you Hans Magnus
Christenson?" I said. "I'm missing a leg. Do you know where
I could find one?" he said. "Yes, I think we could find you one,"
I said. "I would be most grateful," he said. "Are you my
grandfather?" I said. "I have many grandchildren. How would
I know?" he said. "I'm the one who lives in Cincinnati," I said.
"Your name's Tom," he said. "Yes, sir," I said. "You're my
favorite," he said. "Why's that?" I said. "I always wanted
to bomb Cincinnati during the war," he said. "But you weren't
in the war," I said. "I know, that was the trouble," he said.

The Leader

I was sitting on the porch when I watched my neighbors' kids walk by on their way to school. One of them turned and waved to me. I waved back. That's when I realized they were zombies. It scared me at first. How had these little children, so full of life, been conquered by the dead? I never did like those neighbors. Perhaps I should notify the school. It could be contagious. A black and yellow butterfly flew by just then. It swirled and dipped and landed on a flower. Then it flew on, searching, in its random way, for something else. I went in and made myself a glass of ice tea, then came back out and sat down. An old man was sitting on the fire hydrant. I thought about yelling at him, but what was there to say? It wasn't my fire hydrant, after all. A flicker was pecking at the ground. I hadn't seen one in a long time. He pecked until he found a worm. Then he kept searching for more. Hop hop hop. How did he know where to peck? The man on the fire hydrant had risen and was walking down the street. He threw his cane up in the air and caught it. He laughed, then grabbed his heart and fell down. I stood up and was about to jump the railing when he stood up and walked away whistling. I didn't know what had happened. Naturally I thought he had had a heart attack, but I was wrong. About six of those zombie kids jumped out of the bushes and started following him whistling the same tune as the man. I realized he was their leader. They were going nowhere.

The Long Drive

       The odometer on my car was broken so I didn't really
know how far I had gone. But I kept driving, past billboards
and signposts that meant nothing to me. I'd stop every now
and then at a drive-in for coffee. The people I'd meet seemed
strange to me as if they were from another world. Then I'd
be off again, driving who knows where. I'd drive above the
speed limit daring the cops to stop me, but, in truth, I
don't think there were any cops around. It was just flat
prairie as far as the eye could see. But then there were
a few hills, and at times I imagined I could see antelope
grazing far off. I say "I imagined" because they were probably
just stumps of hay. I felt like I was getting closer, but
I didn't really know where that was. I mean, something about
the landscape seemed familiar, like I had been there before,
in a dream, perhaps, the trees, the sky. I drove on and on,
and then it was there. A little cabin off the road hidden by trees,
a long driveway, I was there. I drove up, got out, and knocked.
A little old lady answered. "It's you," I said. "Yes, it's
me," she said. We started to talk. She was lonely, it was
obvious. She had been alone a long time. I felt sorry for
her. She said, "Excuse me," and went into another room. When
she came back she had a gun. She said, "Not this time you
won't."

ii.

Low Flying

   I thought I heard a mouse under the floorboard in my
bedroom. I got down on the floor and pressed my ear to the
floor. Something was scratching there, gnawing, as if it wanted
to eat its way into the room. Maybe it did, I thought
about going down into the basement, but realized it would be
cut off from where the animal was, as well. There was nowhere
it could be viewed. I decided to put it out of my mind.
Hours went by and I felt like I was having my leg chiseled
off. Finally, I went and got a hammer and beat on the floor.
It stopped for a while, then started up elsewhere just as
persistently. I started hammering there and, again, it went
silent. Then it started up again across the floor. I thought
I was going nuts. I decided to get drunk. I got a bottle
of bourbon out of the cabinet and poured myself a drink. When
that was gone I poured myself another. And another. And
another. I was feeling pretty woozy now. When I woke up
in the morning there was a huge hole in my bedroom floor.
I walked around it, aghast, only to find a most peculiar gentle-
man sitting in my living room. "You're probably wondering
what I'm doing here," he said. "Well, I am, too. I was flying
along at a good speed, a bit low, mind you, when I seem to have
entered your crawl space, or whatever it's called. There was
no way out, so I used my teeth. I mean, I had to chew my way out,
if you see what I mean." "I don't at all see what you mean. How
could you be flying so low? And what were you flying in?"
I said. "Yes, yes. These are questions I have been asking
myself," he said. "You don't have any answers?" I said. "No,
I don't have any answers," he said.

The Three Little Boys

The little boy sat there staring at me. We were in the
doctor's office. He had a big lump in his throat. Finally, I
waved to him to come to me. He looked up at his mother. She
said it was okay, so he walked over to me. I reached in my
pocket and pulled out a piece of candy, for which he thanked
me and went running back to his mother. Another kid came in
with a similar ailment, his throat swollen to an impressive
size. He sat with his mother and thumbed through magazines.
The nurse came out and signaled for patients to join her. I
waved to the boy to come over to me. He checked with his
mother to see if it was okay, then he ran over to my side.
I gave him some candy, for which he thanked me, then ran back
to his mother. A third boy came in with his mother shortly
thereafter. He looked like he had a goiter in his throat.
They sat nearby. He picked up a magazine and started to read.
When he looked up I waved him over and gave him a piece of candy.
He thanked me and returned to his mother. I looked at the three
boys around the room and wondered what could have caused their
ailments. They were so similar. I walked up to the first
mother and asked her what was the matter with her son. She
said he swallowed a star. I said, "Oh, my, how did he do that?"
She said she didn't know, but he was sitting on the front steps
one night staring at a star, and when she came back five minutes
later the star was gone and he had a swollen neck. I looked at
the other two mothers. They couldn't have anything to beat this.
So I went to the second one. She said he had swallowed a hedge-
hog. "I'm sorry to hear of that," I said. And the third said
he had swallowed a river, by mistake, of course. A star, a

hedgehog, a river—it didn't make any sense. But looking at the three boys they looked just the same. I concluded, they were the same, just the outlines of their inner intaglio were slightly off. Or maybe not.

The Pearls

      I was reading the evening paper when my wife walked in. She said, "Honey, have you seen my pearl necklace?" "Not since the last time you wore it to the party," I said. "What party was that?" she said. "The Fredicks' party, two weeks ago," I said. "Oh, yes, we had fun, but where could my necklace be? It's not in my jewelry box," she said. "Is it under the bed?" I said. "No, I've looked there," she said. "Well, I don't know," I said. "It didn't fall off at the party. I remember wearing it home. Oh, my," she said. "It will turn up," I said. "I suppose you're right," she said. I went back to reading the paper and Darlene forgot about her pearls and went about doing something else. A while later I said, "Darlene, can you remember the name of the Conroys' boy?" "I think it was Tim, why do you ask?" she said. "There's a piece in the paper about him. He fell off a bridge," I said. "That's terrible. Did he die?" she said. "No, but he broke his neck. He's in Memorial Hospital," I said. "Should we call them, or just send them a card?" she said. "Maybe we should go to the hospital. What do you think?" I said. "We didn't really know him. I think a card would be sufficient," she said. "Okay, if you think so," I said. "Hey, Frank, here's your old cuff link in the corner of the closet," she said. "No kidding, I'd forgotten all about it," I said. "Now you have a pair," she said. "Thanks, sweetheart, I owe you one for that," I said. I read the paper and heard nothing from Darlene for a while. Finally she came out of the bedroom and said, "Whose panties are these?" "I don't know, I've never seen them before," I said. "Well, they aren't mine," she said. "Where did you find them?" I said. "In the pocket of your sports jacket," she said. "Somebody stuck them in there, trying to get me in trouble," I said. "I don't believe you," she said. "Somebody took your pearls and left me their panties, it's as simple as that," I said. "A mouse?" she said. "Yes, a mouse in pearls with no panties," I said.

I Wrote Myself a Letter

       I sat down at my desk and wrote myself a letter. And
then I threw it away. I wrote my grandfather a letter and
I tore that one up also. I wrote my mother a letter, but
I kept that one. I was exhausted. Three letters in one
sitting. I had myself a schnapps. I looked out the window.
It was snowing. A mother and father went jogging up the
street pushing a baby carriage. A hawk was circling
overhead. My grandfather was dead and so was my mother.
But that didn't mean we couldn't communicate. At least
I could share my thoughts with them. They didn't answer,
of course, but that didn't matter. My mother had been a
nurse and, of course, that helped. My grandfather sawed
lumber and that didn't help, but who cared. He was a kind
man. He made model airplanes in his spare time. I went into
the living room and sat down on the sofa. My father ran away
from home when I was three. My mother never told me why.
We never heard from him again. But I don't think about
any of this. It was a beautiful day outside. Three little
mice tiptoed across the lawn. One of them had its arm
in a sling.

The Blue Delusion

The wind kept banging against the door. I thought someone was out there. I got up several times, but no one was there. You don't get used to that kind of thing. Maybe I needed a visitor. By midnight I was tired and went to bed. By morning the wind had died down. I no longer needed a visitor. But, after breakfast, there was a knock on the door. I answered it. It was the police. He said, "Have you seen my ball?" "Your ball?" I said. "Yes, I kicked it over this way and I haven't been able to find it," he said. "Well, no, I haven't seen your ball," I said. "It's red and white, medium sized, and, of course, round. I'd appreciate if you call the station if you find it," he said. "Of course I will. I wouldn't hesitate," I said. I went back and sat down on the couch. A little while later the doorbell rang. It was a policewoman. She said, "Excuse me, but have you seen my doll? I was walking it in its carriage down this street when I saw a burglar and started to run after him. The doll fell out of her carriage around your lawn, I think. It had on diapers and a pink hat. Have you seen her?" "No, but I'll keep an eye out for her and call you if it turns up," I said. "Thank you," she said. And a while later an officer came to the door and said he had lost his toy gun in my yard. "You see, we were playing cops and robbers last night in your backyard and I lost my gun. I don't know how I did it, but I did. I think the robber stole it and then I don't know what happened," he said. "Well, if I find it I'll be sure to call the station," I said. "Better if you call me at home," he said. "Oh, I see. I'll be sure to do that," I said. As soon as he left I called the police station. I said, "Officer, I'm tired of all your officers playing in my yard. I've had three of them so far today." "Mister, I don't know what you're talking about. All of our officers are right here in the office," he said. "But they were here today, I swear it," I said. "Sir, it seems you're suffering from what we call the Blue Delusion. You want them to be playing in your yard. It's common enough. Nothing to worry about," he said. "No, no, no," I cried to myself.

The French Novel

        I am at peace reading on my couch. I am reading a French
novel about a little boy lost in the woods. I pause and sigh.
To be so young and lost, how sad. I get up and go for a glass
of water. I hear a rattling in the attic, no, it's outdoors.
I look out the kitchen window. It's dark, but I can see a buffalo
grazing in my yard. No, it's a cow, only smaller. Maybe it's
a big dog or a wolf. It's a shadow from the tree, then it howls.
It scares me to death with its eerie howling. Then I realize
it's the refrigerator making all that noise. I go back to the
couch and fall asleep. I sleep for an hour and am woken by a
knocking on the door. I rub my eyes, get up, and go to the door.
There's nobody there. I go back to the couch, pick up my book, and
start reading. The boy drinks from a stream, eats walnuts, and keeps
walking. He is still lost. He recognizes nothing. I feel supremely
comfortable. I like being with this boy. He doesn't panic, he
is not afraid, he's centered. Centered? What does that mean?
He stops by a stream and drinks. He takes a nap. When he wakes
it's raining. Nearby he finds a cave. He starts to explore it.
It's huge. And dark. He feels along the walls with his hands.
There are bats sleeping all along the ceiling. There are stalagmites.
Stalactites. Suddenly he sees a clear pool in the middle of the
cave. He walks up to it, looks down. There is no bottom. It
seems to go on forever. I put the book down, wanting the suspense
to go on forever. I picked it up again and a monster jumped out
of the pool and ate the boy.

That's Not My Duty

The man looked at me funny. I said, "What's wrong with you?" He said, "Probably lots of things, but I'm just here to make sure you do your duty." I said, "What do you mean 'my duty'?" "Surely you know what I mean when I refer to your duty," he said. "Actually, I don't. It sounds like some very particular thing," I said. "I thought you had agreed to do it. That was my understanding when I came here," he said. "Well, if I had agreed to do it, I no longer remember what it was," I said. "We don't have many cases like this. Normally, if a person agrees to do something they remember," he said. "Perhaps your bookkeeping is amiss. Perhaps it was another person with my name. Some kind of error on your part," I said. "It has happened, but it is very rare. We make very few errors," he said. "I know I would remember something involving duty. That's such a serious word," I said. "Perhaps you've fallen down and hit your head. Maybe someone's punched you. It could have been erased in all kinds of ways. Why don't you just accept it now?" he said. "No, I don't think I will. I don't like the way it has come up," I said. "But it's your duty," the man said. "It is not," I said. "I have it written down on paper," he said. "I don't care," I said. "I'm going to report you to the commissioner," he said. "Go ahead and report me," I said. He slammed the door and walked out to his car and drove away. I felt really good about my life. I wasn't indebted to anyone. Just then Cindy called and said, "I want you to wear a hat this evening." And I thought, yes, no, yes, no. She said, "What do you say to that?" And I said, "Of course I will wear a hat."

The Aquatic Ape

The river was high due to the recent rains. I walked above
it. Sometimes boats would pass and people waved. I rarely saw
anybody on this walk. It was a pretty day in May. There were
wildflowers along the banks. Overhead hawks circled. I saw
a man coming toward me. He had on a hat and wore a beard and
carried a large walking stick. He was not anybody I knew. When
he came abreast of me he said, "I'd be careful if I were you.
Something was chasing me back there. It had a loud growl and was
very fast. I never did see what it was." "It could
have been a wolf," I said. "I think it came out of the river,"
he said. "Then I don't know what it might have been," I said.
"Some kind of aquatic ape," he said. "I've never heard of such
a thing," I said. "Maybe it's a new thing," he said. "Something
like that doesn't just start up," I said. "It's got to start
somewhere," he said. "Well, anyway it didn't get you," I said.
"Not yet. It could follow me home," he said. "Or it could eat
me and be satisfied," I said. "That's why you better not go down
there," he said. "But I was so looking forward to this walk.
I haven't taken it in quite a while," I said. "You take it
today and it may very well be your last time," he said. "I
won't take it. It breaks my heart, but I won't," I said. "This
thing was very angry and it was trying to kill me," he said.
"It's always been such a peaceful walk for me," I said. "Now
it's a living hell," he said. "I'm sorry," I said. He tipped
his hat to me and walked away. An aquatic ape, I thought, that's
a good one. I've got to see this, and walked further down the
path.

Some Things I Need

I said I was tired and didn't want to hear about it. Megan
put on her bathrobe and walked to the window. "Well, I'm tired,
too, but there are certain things that need talking about," she
said. "Surely they can wait until tomorrow," I said. "No, we need
to talk about these things right now," she said. "Okay, if it's
so urgent, I will sit up and pinch myself awake. How's that?"
I said. "Now, Jack, if we buy this boat tomorrow that you're talking
about, where are we going to store it?" "I'm going to rent a pier
right down there on Stony Bay," I said. "How many times a year do
you think we'll take it out?" she said. "I don't know, maybe three
or four," I said. "Boats always need repairs, did you figure that
into the overall costs?" she said. "I haven't added any of this
up. I admit I have no idea what the overall costs will be," I
said. "I just wanted you to think about it before we jumped in,"
she said. Then we went to sleep. When we woke up in the morning,
I said, "Let's go get the monkey." She said, "What monkey? What
are you talking about?" "I saw a monkey at the pet store.
It'll be much easier to take care of than a boat. It costs less
and we can keep it in the house," I said. She said, "I don't
want a monkey. It would be screeching all the time and make a
mess. You must be crazy," she said. "It's very cute and sweet,
and it can wear disposable diapers," I said. "We're not getting
a monkey. That's all there is to it," she said. I felt very sad,
of course. A monkey was so very different than a boat. It had
no sails to be torn in the wind. It had no rudder to be scraped
on the beach. It was the perfect opposite of the sailboat, and
yet she disliked both. Megan was not easy to live with. But
I loved Megan. I put up with her eccentricities. I bought a
boa constrictor and kept it under the bed. It was large enough
to swallow us both.

Buddha

I lay on the couch reading my book when the doorbell rang.
I got up and went to the door. I opened it. There was the post-
man with a large package in his hand. I greeted him and signed
for the package. I didn't know what it was. I took it inside
and laid it on the table. I got a knife from the drawer and
started to open it. When I took it out of the packing there was a large
statue of Buddha inside. I set it on the table and stepped back
to admire it. It was quite beautiful, though I couldn't figure
out why anybody would send it to me. I thought no more about it
and went back to reading my book. A while later Perry called me.
He said, "Did you get my Buddha?" I said, "Yes, but I didn't know
you sent it." "Don't worry about that. I'll be by in a while to
pick it up," he said. "But I like it," I said. "Don't worry
about that. I'll get you another one," he said. I felt perturbed,
but I didn't know what to do about it. I went back to reading
my book. I fell asleep on the couch and dreamed of Buddha saving
my life. I was in a tree with tigers all around me. Buddha
came and tamed the tigers. I climbed down and petted them. Then
there was a knock on the door. I woke up and answered it. Perry
said, "How are you doing? I've come for the Buddha." "But you
sent it to me. I thought it was a present," I said. "I told you,
I'll get you another one," he said. "But I like this one," I said.
"You can't have this one. This one's special," he said. "But
that's what I like about it," I said. "I'm sorry, Frank. I have
to have this one. I'll get you one that looks just like it," he
said. "But, Perry, this one means a lot to me," I said. "This
one is packed with dope. You don't want that, do you, Frank?" he
said. I froze and turned away. I thought of all the good he had

done for me in my dream. And now to think he was smuggling dope. "Take him away," I said. "He's yours." Perry grabbed him and carried him out the door. I said, "Perry, I don't want another one." He said, "Why not?" "You never know where they've been," I said. He laughed and drove off. I stood there and stared at the sunset.

To Russia with Love

I was told the package had already been sent to Moscow
and there was nothing I could do about it. I said, "What about
all the paperwork?" The manager said, "Yes, that too. But if
you would like to take a look at it, it can be arranged." I said,
"Oh, no, I trust your people." I went back to my office and
started playing a video game. Mr. Stewart stuck his head in my
office and said, "Is everything okay, I mean, with the package
to Moscow?" "It's going its way," I said. "And the paperwork?"
he said. "Yes, yes, everything's taken care of," I said. "It's
just that this is very important," he said. "I've checked on
everything," I said. "It has to be there tomorrow night," he
said. "Yes, I know," I said. I had lost interest in the video
game. I took it out and put it away. A new secretary stuck her
head in my door. "Mr. Mercer, I'm afraid you're not going to
like this, but I've discovered that that package you sent to
Moscow has been sent to Moscow, Idaho, and not Moscow, Russia,"
she said. "Oh, no, this is dreadful. Russia is expecting it
tomorrow. What are we going to do?" I said. "Well, you could send
me to Idaho on the next flight out, but still I don't know if
that would give us enough time," she said. "It's the only chance
we've got. You must go," I said. "Mr. Mercer, would you come with
me? I'm afraid of flying," she said. "Well, of course, Charlene.
I can be ready to go in five minutes," I said. I went and told
the boss what had happened and what we were going to do about it.
He was staring out the window when I told him. Then he swung
around and looked at me. "Do you know what was in that box, Mr.
Mercer?" he said. I said I did not. "It was just a box of old
fish heads," he said. "They wanted something to fix their biggest

rocket and that's what we sent them." "Fish heads?" I said. "Yes, they can fix anything," he said. I went back to the new secretary and said, "I don't think we're going anywhere." She said, "Why?" I said, "Fish heads." "Oh, I love fish heads," she said.

The Goddess

I saw the goddess up ahead in her broken-down jalopy. I
managed to get just behind her. She stuck her arm out straight
to indicate that she was turning left on Roosevelt Street. I
did the same and followed her down the street of broken-down
shacks and hovels. She stopped in front of one of them and got
out and checked the mail. Then she went inside. I had stopped
a little in back of her, not knowing what I wanted. I sat there
and stared at the house. After about fifteen minutes I walked up
to the door. She answered. "Yes, what is it?" she said. "It's
hard to explain," I said. "I followed you from town. I thought
maybe you might be an angel, and I wanted to talk to you." "Well,
I'm sorry to disappoint you. I'm afraid I'm nothing like an
angel. In fact, I'm barely a human being. I take the garbage
out of restaurants. I spend most of my time at the dump looking
for things," she said. "I still think you're an angel. You've
just fallen a few notches. Why don't you let me take you out
to a restaurant sometime?" I said. "You would be terribly dis-
appointed. I know I am," she said. "No, I wouldn't be. I'm
very excited just talking to you," I said. "There's something
wrong with you. You don't see who I am. I am a monster of garbage,"
she said. "No, you're lovely. I think you're beautiful," I
said. "You're crazy. Please go away. I must eat my gruel and
sleep if I am to work tomorrow," she said. "Let me save you.
You must quit that job. I will get you another. I promise I
will change your life," I said. "Why would I do that? This is
my life," she said. "You deserve better," I said. She slammed
the door and locked it. I stood there with my hand in the air.
Then I turned and walked back to the car. I had seen a goddess,
but she had gotten away. She was just too fast for me.

Beer for the Fairies

Two Clydesdale horses were pulling a heavy wagon full of barrels right through the center of town. The driver wore bib overalls and had a white beard. Several drivers were yelling at him to get out of the way, but the driver didn't acknowledge them. When the light changed he yelled at the horses, but they took their time. I was standing by the side of the street watching all this. The driver looked as if he had been doing this all his life. Without thinking about what I was doing I ran out and jumped on the wagon. It's a small town and so, even at that slow pace, soon we were out of it. We turned off the main drag onto a dirt road and it got pretty bumpy. The driver still didn't seem to know I was accompanying him. One bump nearly threw me off and I let out a little cry. We went down a steep hill at a pretty good pace and the kegs were starting to roll around. I stopped them from rolling out of the wagon when I could. We traveled through a forest where it was almost dark. Deer scampered away at our approach. I was questioning what I was doing there. As close as it was to town I had never been there before. I had lost all sense of direction. Suddenly, the horses stopped. Little fairy men came out of the trees and started to unload the wagon. They didn't see me or speak to me. They gleefully shouldered the kegs and marched into the dark woods and then returned for more. I couldn't tell how many of them there were, six or eight. The one to take the last keg stopped and looked at me. "We like your beer very much. Someday we will make it ourselves, but it is still a mystery. I hope you are having a nice day. Good-bye," he said. Then he handed the driver a bag of something. The driver turned the horses around and we headed back. When we got to the middle of town I jumped off. Daniel saw me. He said, "What were you doing on that thing?" "I was helping out with a delivery," I said. "What kind of delivery?" he said. "Beer for the fairies," I said. "Oh, that makes sense," he said.

The Moose

I lay there in the grass and pretended I had been shot by
an Indian. Of course there were no Indians around. Then I heard
a shot fired and I sat up. I looked around. I didn't see any-
one. I stood up and walked around. I didn't see anyone. I still
didn't see anyone. I walked around the yard. Then I went into
the house and mixed myself some lemonade. I went out onto the porch
and sat down. I heard another shot. A moose ran across my
front yard. A hunter ran out of the woods. I yelled, "Don't fire.
This is a residential neighborhood." He turned and looked at me.
"Did you see that moose?" he said. "Why, yes, I saw him," I said.
"It had my name written on it," he said. "No, it had my neighbor-
hood written on it. Now you go away or I'll call the police," I
said. He walked back in the woods and disappeared. After a while
the moose came back into my yard and just stared at me. I said,
"Do you want a glass of lemonade?" It started eating my flower
garden. I said, "Stop that!" It kept on eating. I said, "Please
stop eating my flowers." It looked up at me. I said, "I really
wish you would stop that." It went on eating. I grabbed a big
board from the porch and went outside. The moose looked at me.
Then it charged me and sent me flying. As I lay on my back I
moved one limb, then another. I didn't seem to have anything
broken. Slowly I rose to my feet. I could barely stand. I wiggled
this way and that. I looked around. There was no moose in sight.
My neighbor, Ted, walked over. "Are you all right? I saw that
through my bedroom window. I couldn't believe it," he said. "Oh,
that was just an imaginary moose. It wasn't a real one," I said.
"No, I saw it. It was real all right," he said. "For you, maybe,
but not for me. It was just a mental thing," I said. I took
a few steps, then crumpled to the ground.

The Encyclopedia Salesman

I went walking up the driveway of Edward Mulcahy. I was going to try to sell him a set of encyclopedias. A dog started barking at me. Mrs. Mulcahy came to the door. "He won't hurt you. He's just pretending to guard the house, but really he wants to be your friend," she said. "I have something I want to show you," I said. "Well, come on up, don't be afraid," she said. "I'm selling encyclopedias," I said. "Well, aren't you the man?" she said. I walked up onto her porch, the dog still sniffing around my ankles. "I have a twelve-volume set that normally sells for $328, but is marked down to $249 for just this week. Within these twelve volumes you will find anything and everything you ever wanted to know," I said. "Would you like to come into the house? I could make you a cup of tea," she said. "Why, thank you," I said. While she was making the tea she said, "When I am sleeping at night I often have the feeling that something is sucking on my little toe. What is that called?" "I'm afraid I don't know," I said. "Or, when you're in one room and you hear a conversation through the wall, and then you go in the other room and no one's there, is there a name for that?" she said. "I don't know of one," I said. She served us tea. We sat at a table in the kitchen. "This encyclopedia has all the most up-to-date knowledge in the world. Over twelve hundred scholars and historians have contributed to it. It is an invaluable source of knowledge," I said. "There is a ghost that lives in here with my husband and me. He only appears periodically, and then always after dark. He speaks to us, but I can't understand a word he says. My husband thinks he speaks Aramaic, says he wants to trade things, but how can you trade with a ghost?" she said. "I don't know. Anyway, you can look up almost any subject in the encyclopedia and there will be a full entry, all the latest answers to your questions," I said. "I walk around all day feeling there is something missing. I don't know what it is, but nothing seems complete without it. Even when my husband's here, I feel it, some crack in the fabric of our being. Do you know what that's called?" she said. "Everything is in here," I said. "Like right now," she said, "I feel that God has flown away and left us to ponder our crimes. Who has done what to whom? No one knows the answers. Everyone is pointing fingers. Then night falls and we are alone." "It's all in here," I said.

The Holman Dairy

       One of the cows had exploded out at the Holman farm. I decided to drive out and see what I could find out. There were a number of policemen there, plus a few reporters. Holman himself was trying to clean the place up. The police kept saying, "We might want that as evidence. Why don't you leave that for us to do?" Holman paid them no mind. He swept and cleaned, and gathered the parts. I was standing in the corner by the head of the cow. "What do you think happened?" a reporter asked Holman. But Holman wouldn't talk to the reporter. He just kept sweeping and scrubbing. I stepped over the head and walked out into the field. There must have been a hundred cows out there. They were eating hay. A little boy walked up to me. "Why are you looking at our cows?" he said. "Didn't you hear? One of them exploded," I said. "Oh, that's not such a big deal. One of them is exploding all the time," he said. "Why do you think that is?" I said. "It's the nature of cows," he said. "But I've never heard of it before," I said. "You never lived with cows," he said. "So you've had many of them explode on you before?" I said. "Two or three a season I suppose," he said. "Why have we never heard of it before?" I asked. "Father doesn't like to advertise. He's afraid it would scare away customers," he said. "Oh, I understand that. I won't tell anybody," I said. "He'd have to kill you," the boy said. "He'd do that?" I said. "Well, it's our dairy farm," the boy said. "Yes, I understand that. I won't tell anybody," I said. "One day we'll find out what's causing it," he said. "Yes, I'm sure you will," I said. I walked back up to the road where I'd parked my car. I got in and drove back to town. I went to the post office to mail a package. The man behind the counter said, "Did you hear about the Holman Family Farm?" I said, "No, I never heard anything." "All their cows are exploding. They say the people who drank their milk are going to explode, too. It's an awful mess," he said. I mailed my package and walked out of there, trying to remember whether or not I had drunk their milk. I couldn't remember. Nonetheless, I felt something ticking inside of me.

The Friars Club Fellow

I was standing on the corner of Forest and Green. A man walked by wearing a three-piece suit and a bowtie. He stopped and looked at me. He said, "You're in the Friars Club, aren't you?" I said, "I've never belonged to the Friars Club, but I hear they are a real nice bunch of fellows." "Nice doesn't begin to cover it. They'll die for you," he said. "Well, I don't want anybody getting hurt over me, but I appreciate the enthusiasm," I said. "I don't think you're our type," he said. "No, I'm probably not," I said. "Sorry for disturbing you," he said. "That's all right. No harm done," I said. "Well, there's harm done to me, I mean, in my misjudgment of you. How I could have ever thought you were a Friars man is a blot on my judgment that I will carry with me the rest of my life," he said. "Isn't that a bit severe? I mean, we had barely met. There are a thousand things I could have been, a juggler, a brick mason, a bike rider. Friars Club members are a very small thing compared to the rest of the world," I said. "I never thought of it like that before. Excuse me, I must be leaving," he said. "No, I don't want you to leave," I said. "But I must leave," he said. "What in the hell do Friars do?" I said. "They do good for other people. That is their sole objective in life," he said. "A lot of people say that," I said. "People say all kinds of things, but Friars are good for their word," he said. "Then I want to be a Friar," I said. "No, you can't be one," he said. "Why not?" I said. "Because I say so," he said. He walked across the street on a red light. A cement truck narrowly missed him. He turned to wave to me and bumped into a streetlight and crumpled onto the ground.

The Orchid

The moon was bright that night. The air was crisp. I
sat on the porch and nearly froze to death. I was waiting for
Armand. He had the information I needed before I could go any
further. It got to be eleven o'clock. Finally his car pulled
up. I got up and went inside. At the door he said, "Sorry
I'm late. I had another appointment." "That's okay, come on
in." We sat down in the living room. "How are you, Armand?"
I said. "I've never been better. And yourself, Jeff?" he
said. "Oh, I've been better, but I'm all right," I said. "It's
lovely out here in the country," he said. "Yes, it's quite
nice," I said. "Well, let's get down to business. What exactly
is it that you would like to know?" he said. "What do you feed
your Teresópolis?" I said. "You're a tricky fellow, aren't you?
I don't usually talk about my Teresópolis, but since we're all
alone in the middle of the country I don't see how it would do
any harm. I give my Teresópolis one fried egg and two sausages
once a month, lots of strawberry Kool-Aid in between, a bologna
sandwich now and then, some vanilla ice cream, a rattlesnake . . ."
"A rattlesnake? Where am I going to get that?" I said. "In
your backyard. There's always one lurking somewhere, you just
have to look," he said. "All this for an orchid?" I said. "They're
very beautiful. My mother cried when hers blossomed," he said.
"But why the rattlesnake?" I said. "It gives them that special
edge to fight off the shakes, put a little color in their cheeks,"
he said. "Well, I can't argue with that. I certainly want it
to be happy," I said. "If it's not you'll be sorry," he said.
"What do you mean by that?" I said. "You'll see," he said.

Possible Suspects

I saw my name on a list of possible suspects. It made me furious. I drove down to the police station immediately. I walked in and the first officer I saw stopped me. I said, "Why is my name on this list? I have done nothing illegal. I want my name removed right now." "Slow down, buster. You sound just like all the guilty ones. I don't know who made this up, but they must have had some reason to put you on it," he said. "I am a law-abiding citizen. I pay my taxes. I follow the speed limit. I don't molest children. I don't rob banks," I said. "You sound like you're not having any fun at all," he said. "I listen to the radio. I make pancakes," I said. "You're pathetic," he said. "About once a year I go bowling," I said. "This is the saddest story I've heard since my grandpa died," he said. "Occasionally I go out to eat at Sal's Diner," I said. "I hate the place. They got bugs in their rice," he said. "I once volunteered for the March of Dimes," I said. "A bunch of phonies," he said. "You don't like me. You don't like anything I do," I said. "Do I look like I care what you do? I don't care even a tiny bit. I got my own fish to fry," he said. "You got fish to fry?" I said. "Trout," he said. "I love trout. That's my favorite fish," I said. "I'm not going to invite you to dinner. I have little kids," he said. "I love little kids," I said. "You love every-thing, because you have nothing." "That's right," I said, "because I have nothing."

The Seafaring Boy

A small office boy by the name of Quinon failed to show up
one day. I sent a message to his home, but there was no reply.
He was not there the next day, so after work I took my bicycle
and rode my way to his home. When I knocked on the door, the mother
replied. She said she had not seen her boy in two days. I asked
her if she had any idea where he might have gone. She said her
boy loved the sea, but she had no idea how he might have gotten
there. I thanked her very much and left. On the way home I
realized I should have asked her if there was a special place on
the sea he knew best. I couldn't just go chasing after the sea.
I got home and found him sleeping on my couch. In the morning
he asked me if I could loan him some money. I asked him, "What
for?" "So I can go to the seashore," he said. "And what is waiting
for you at the seashore?" I said. "I don't know. It's just important
that I go," he said. "Okay, but come back, will you?" I said.
"Yes, I'll come back," he said. He took off before I went to
work. I went to work wondering about what I had done. Two weeks
passed, then three. I had stopped thinking about the boy. We
had hired a new office boy and things were going along just fine.
One day I got home from work and there was a note in the mail
that said, "I have hired out on a ship that is going around the
world—Quinon." I called his mother and told her. She cried and
cried and cried. I said, "Why don't you come over?" And she
said, "No."

The Blue Ones

A motor vehicle rumbled down the road up above where
we were hiding. It went on down the road and we resumed
our hiking. A deer dashed in front of us and we gave a start.
We were hiding from the law because we felt like it. We
hadn't really done anything wrong, but we felt we had.
We just took off hiking one day and said we didn't want to be
caught by the law. We camped every night and hiked all day,
and the more we hiked the more we felt the need to escape.
I said to Alan one day, "Do you think they're near?" He said,
"Who's they?" "The cops, stupid," I said. "Oh, the cops,
sure they're near. They're right on our tails," he said.
"What should we do?" I said. "Duck and run," he said. Then
I spotted something blue darting through the green of the
forest. "I think we had better duck," I said. So we found a
hole and lay down as best we could. We watched and waited.
After a half an hour we crept forward and stopped. "I think
I see another one up there," Roscoe said. We lowered ourselves
to the ground. The blue one came near us. He aimed his pistol
and fired. It went right over our heads. "Let's get out of
here," I whispered, and we started running uphill and
more shots were fired. Finally, Roscoe took one in the arm.
He held his handkerchief to his arm and kept running. Then
I caught one in the chest and fell down. Roscoe came back
for me and I said, "No, keep going." Then they shot him dead
right there. He fell over onto me. Three of them walked
up to me and shot me dead. "For what?" were my last words.

The New Opera

This was a special occasion for us because, well, we
hadn't been out in a while. It was a party to celebrate the
opening of the opera. I had no idea why we were invited
because, frankly, we had never been to the opera. As we
were standing there a lady came up to me and said, "I thought
your sister was magnificent in *Aida*. She really stole the
show." "Why, thank you," I said. My wife looked at me as if
I were crazy. "You have no sister," she whispered. "I know,
but we must be polite," I said. We mingled with the people
as if we belonged. Before long a gentleman came up and said,
"Your daughter was divine in *Don Juan*." "Thank you, thank you
very much," I said. We had a drink and my wife said, "This
isn't so bad." "I'm rather enjoying it," I said. A woman was
eyeing me from a short distance away. Finally she came over
and said, "Can I have your autograph?" "Why certainly," I said.
She said, "On my breast," and handed me the pen. When she left
my wife glowered at me, then said, "Your fame is growing." "I
can't wait to see what's next," I said. A crowd started to
gather around me. One young man stepped forward and said,
"Are you the new president of the opera association?" I
hesitated, then said, "I'm afraid not." "I don't believe you,
you're just too modest." A crowd started to gather. "Speech!
Speech!" they yelled. I looked at my wife. She looked
something between amused and terrified. I walked up onto
the small stage and said, "My fellow opera lovers, it is my
sad duty to inform you that opera is dead. It will never
be heard again." Just then a huge man dove at me and knocked

me to the floor. A fight broke out on the stage. I crawled
away and stood up and ran to my wife. "Let's go," I said.
When we got outside, my wife said, "Why did you say that?"
"It was just part of the new show," I said.

Brand New Mantra

Further along the road there was a bright red bush
on the right side and a pine tree on the left. Then there was
a little bridge that crossed the creek. There was a hole in the
ground where bees came and went, and wildflowers sprinkled
the ground here and there. I found a log by the side of the
road and sat down to eat my lunch. Earlier in the day I had
seen a fox cross the road. My lunch consisted of a bologna
sandwich and some chips. I had walked seven miles so far
that day. My lunch tasted good. When I was finished, I
lay down on the log and napped. When I woke, the ground
was covered with a soft, silver lining. Sunlight. I walked
on. There was a grape arbor up ahead. The road spun around
and around. I disappeared in the spinning. I woke up and
started walking again. I walked into a wall and slid down.
I got up and started walking again. When I got to the grape
arbor I plucked a grape. Then another. And another. I ate
myself sick. But I kept going, stopping now and again to
smell a flower. Then I was stung by a bee and I fell
down a hole and I was surrounded by bees, who kept saying my
name, like a mantra they had just learned.

Almost a Saint

I said to my wife, "Why don't you come here for a minute." She came and I showed her the upside-down label on the can of soup. "What do you think this means?" I said. "It must be some kind of poison," she said. "I'm going to open it," I said. "It might explode," she said. "I don't think so," I said. So I opened it. There was a dead mouse inside the can. My wife jumped back, nearly fainted. "How the hell did this get in the can?" I said. "Somebody had to put it there," she said. "What a sick joke," I said. "That person deserves to be shot," she said. "They'll never find him," I said. "The perfect crime," she said. "Should we report it to someone?" I said. "Nobody would care," she said. "How about the government?" I said. "What are they going to do?" she said. "They could fine them a million dollars," I said. "And what about us? We're the ones who had to suffer the shock," she said. "We get nothing," I said. I was still holding the can with the mouse in it. I didn't know what to do with it. "And that million dollars will buy a toilet seat for the army," she said. I didn't want to throw it away, and I couldn't just put it on a shelf. "It doesn't seem right to just forget it, pretend it never happened," I said. "What do you want to do, call our friends and form a parade down Main Street?" she said. "No, I want to pray," I said. "You what?" she said. "I said I want to pray for the soul of the mouse," I said. "Get out of here," she said. "I'm serious. He never hurt anybody, and look how he died. He was practically a saint. It makes me want to cry," I said. "Here, give me the can. I'll flush him down the toilet," she said.

Dangerous at Night

I was told not to go into the park after dark as it was
filled with drug addicts and thieves. However, there was a
full moon out and I wanted to sit by the river. I knew there
were benches by the river. I was a little afraid, but not too
much. There were great old oaks lining the sidewalk. Every now
and then I saw a pair of lovers, but mostly the park seemed
empty. I walked past a broken fountain where a drunk was passed
out. There were some crushed beer cans on the sidewalk. Azalea
bushes were in bloom. And, finally, the river with the moonlight
playing on its surface. It was more beautiful than I had imagined.
I found a bench and sat down. I was very glad I had come. There
was a light breeze rustling the leaves in the trees. I hadn't
a thought in the world, when a man walked up behind me and said,
"This is a stickup. Give me all of your money or I'll kill you."
I said, "Have you ever seen anything so beautiful? A full moon
always makes me very happy. How about you?" "I've got a gun
pointed at your head. Are you crazy? Now give me all of your
money," he said. "I had heard this park was dangerous at night,
but then I came out and I found this. I think a full moon is
lucky. I think this is my lucky night," I said. "You think a
bullet in your head is lucky? Because that's what you're going
to get if you don't hand over your wallet fast," he said. "Why
don't you sit down? You seem tense. I could give you a back rub.
Maybe that would help," I said. "What's wrong with you? Don't
you understand that I have a gun to your head?" he said. "Sir,
can't you see that this is a most extraordinary moment? Can't
you just drop your old ways and look at what's before you? We

may never see this again. The beauty of it brings tears to my eyes. Just look," I said. "Yes, I see, but I'm trying to hold you up," he said. "Sit down, for God's sake. We are brothers under this moonlight. Can't you see that?" I said.

In the Lake

I sat down by the lake and skipped a couple of rocks.
Then I lay down on the grass and closed my eyes. I slept
a little. I don't know how long because I had forgotten my
watch. But when I opened my eyes I sensed someone was watching
me. I stood up and looked around. I didn't see anyone. Finally,
a little old lady stepped out of the woods. "You must follow
me," she said. "Why?" I said. "Because you must," she said.
She turned around and headed into the woods. I shook my head and
followed her. She made her way through the thick bramble and
bushes quite skillfully. I seemed to have more trouble.
Every now and then she'd turn her head and say, "Hurry up.
What's wrong with you?" I was going as fast as I could. Then
I twisted my foot on a rock and was limping. My foot hurt
pretty badly. But I was trying to keep up with her. We headed
down a steep ravine and then climbed a hill. I was out of
breath, but she kept going. We crossed a plain of nettle bushes.
My arms and legs were bleeding. "Please slow down," I said,
but she didn't. Finally she stopped at a little cabin on a
hillside. "This is where I live," she said. "It's nice," I said.
"Come inside," she said. I followed her in. It was attractively
furnished with antiques. "Come over here," she said. I walked
over to the bedroom. There was a dead man in the bed. "You
must take him and dump him in the lake," she said. "I could
never carry him that far, with all of the ups and downs," I said.
"I have a wheelbarrow you can use. There's another way that's
mostly flat," she said. "Why don't you have him buried?" I said.
"Oh, I have no money for that. Will you do this for me?" she
said. "I'll try," I said. I picked him up. He couldn't have

weighed more than ninety pounds. She went and got the wheelbarrow.
Then gave me the directions. She said she couldn't come because
it made her too sad. I pushed off and headed for the lake.
It was flat for the most part. Still, my arms ached. I had
to pause now and then. When I got to the lake I tried to find
the deepest part near the shore. Then I dumped him. He floated
at first, but then he slowly sank. I returned the wheelbarrow
to the old lady. She said, "How will I ever live without
Albert?" "Oh, you'll find a way," I said. "He was everything
to me," she said. "You can visit him at the lake," I said.
Her eyes glazed over and she slumped in her chair, so I
took my leave. I wanted to go home as quickly as possible,
but I got lost again and again. Everything seemed to be in
the wrong place.

The Llama

  Sanjoo Huh called on his cell phone to tell me he was
on a llama riding through the mountains in search of the girl
who had been kidnapped last week. I said, "Where did you get
the llama?" He said, "I think the girl is sleeping in a tent
or a little cabin. A strong man is guarding her. I will tell
him I am a miner and, then, when we are having tea or whiskey,
I will surprise him and hack him to bits." "Where did you get
the llama?" I said. "I will carry her down the mountain to safety.
Her parents have offered a reward, but I'm not so sure I want
it. Don't you think it would be tacky of me to accept it?" he
said. "If you really needed the money, that would be one thing.
But you don't need it, Sanjoo. A little good publicity is in-
valuable," I said. "I'm not doing it for publicity. I'm doing
it to help out the girl," he said. "Sanjoo," I said, "I can
barely hear you. Your cell phone is breaking up. Try me again
later." On the local news that night I heard that the girl had
been found in a local garage somewhere. She was okay, a few scratches
here and there, but okay. The reward was paid to some teenager
who was happy as hell to receive it. I didn't know where Sanjoo
was so I couldn't tell him. He called a couple of days later
to say he was spying on the culprits and was about to make his
move. I said, "Sanjoo, they found the girl. She's okay. You
can come back now." He said, "No, I will have her in no time.
You can prepare the celebration for me." I said, "The girl is
fine. She is back with her family." "I am going to sneak up
on them and club them. I am not even afraid. I feel certain
that God is with me," he said. Then the signal broke up again.
When I didn't hear from Sanjoo in the next few days I reported

him missing to the police. I told them what I knew of his last whereabouts, which wasn't much. I thought about him constantly. Weeks, and then months went by. I missed him incredibly and assumed the worst. Then one day I saw him sitting in a restaurant by himself. I ran in and embraced him. He said, "Dan, is that you?" "Well, of course it's me. Where have you been? I've been worried sick about you," I said. "My llama took me to Peru. He had a brother there that he hadn't seen in a long time," he said. "Did you find him?" I said. "Of course not. Everybody looks like a llama in Peru," he said.

The Great Wall

Maureen was looking through a magazine on the couch. I
asked her if she wanted some lemonade. She said, "Sure." So
I went into the kitchen and made some up. I brought her a glass.
I was drinking some, too. I said, "You look especially nice
today." She said, "It must be my new hairdo. Robert insisted
on giving me this new flip." "Well, I like it, whatever he did,"
I said. "He says he's going on this expedition to Antarctica.
He says he wants to see a whole colony of penguins in their native
state," she said. "It's a lot easier to just go to the zoo,"
I said. "He's very eccentric," she said. "I'd call that worse
than eccentric," I said. "Did you read this article about the
Great Wall of China?" she said. "No," I said. "It was built
to keep the Mongols out. They were savage, brutal people. It
took hundreds of years to build, all different kinds of material,"
she said. "They should make a movie about it," I said. "Or we
could go there and see it for ourselves," she said. "I would
probably fall off the Wall," I said. "Oh, Harry, I wish you
wouldn't think of yourself that way," she said. "You know I
don't like heights," I said. "Then we won't go," she said.
"I would drive the Trans-Canada Highway," I said. "Why?"
she said. "Because it's on the ground," I said. "I want to
finish the Great Wall, if you don't mind," she said. "No, I
don't mind. I'll go out and weed the garden," I said. I gathered
some garden tools and went outside. I looked at the garden. It
didn't really need weeding. I had weeded it yesterday. So
I just walked around the yard. There was an eagle circling
overhead. A little man in a suit walked out of the woods.
"Is there a cemetery around here?" he said. "It's just down

the street," I said. "My wife's buried there. She fell out of an airplane. She was walking on the wing when a gull hit her," he said. "Why was she walking on the wing?" I said. "No one ever explained that to me," he said. "Maybe that was her dream," I said. "Could be. She was a wild one," he said. "What were you doing in the woods?" I said. "Hunting bear," he said. "But you don't have a gun," I said. "I was hunting them with my hands," he said. "I see you didn't get any," I said. "Well, I'm not going to carry a bear all the way to the cemetery, am I?" he said. "No, of course not," I said.

The Interrupted Flow

Grover swung on a rope. Harvey caught him and Grover said, "What do you think you're doing? I was only halfway through my arc. You've interrupted my natural flow." "I thought you were going to crash. I was only trying to protect you," Harvey said. Grover slumped into a pile and said, "Well, that is my last try. I gave it everything I could. Now I am defeated." "You should be thanking me for your life. If you had kept going like that I honestly believe you might have died," Harvey said. "But I'd be a hero. People would be talking about me. Eventually there'd be a statue," Grover said. "A little tiny statue that nobody would see," Harvey said. "Now you're being cruel. Why would you want to hurt me?" Grover said. "Wake up, old boy, you're alive. What could be better than that?" Harvey said. Grover crawled around on the ground. "I'm looking for a stick," he said. "Why would you want a stick?" Harvey said. "I want a stick to poke you," he said. "Why would you want to poke me?" Harvey said. "I want you to know how it feels to have all the air let out of you," Grover said. "Come on, let's be friends," Harvey said. "You stopped me from the greatness I was born to achieve. That's hardly the basis for friendship," he said. "I kept you alive. Doesn't that count for anything?" Harvey said. "You kept me from immortality. Now I am just a snail crawling along a path waiting to be crushed," he said. "Escargot is my favorite appetizer," Harvey said. "You wicked fiend," Grover said.

Lost at Sea

One day I said to the captain, "Do you have any idea where we are?" He said, "Of course not. I haven't any idea." "Then perhaps we ought to turn back," I said. "Back where? Ever since I broke my toy compass we've been lost. It's all the same to me," he said. "Well, we've got to do something," I said. "I'll do anything," he said. "Follow a gull," I said. "Why would I follow a gull?" he said. "Because they fly back to land," I said. "Yes, that's a good idea," he said. But we didn't see any gulls. We were spinning in circles. "Go in a straight line," I told him. "Yes, a straight line. That's a good idea," he said. We went in a straight line for a long time. I was starting to lose hope. "I feel good about this. I think we'll find something soon," he said. "Why? We could be on our way to Antarctica," I said. "You must keep your spirits up. I think we're going to be all right," he said. We had some food and drink left, so that was good. A storm came on and high waves nearly turned us over. But then it was gone and calm waters returned and we sailed on. I saw a whale jump and then some dolphins swam by. Finally, I said, "I think we're going to die out here. There are worse ways to go, I suppose." "We're not going to die. I see some-thing up ahead," he said. "Yes, I see something, too. But what is it?" I said. "It could be an island," the captain said. "I don't think so," I said. "Why are you such a pessimist?" he said. "Don't you see? The whole world is hiding from us. We're not a part of anything. We're just flotsam," I said. "I don't believe you for one minute. I don't know where you get such ideas," he said. "There's the Statue of Liberty." "That's a shark and you know it," I said.

The Police Captain's Remorse

I had been beaten and tortured for days. Then one day information arrived that they had been holding the wrong man. The captain let me go. He apologized for all the inconvenience, as he put it. He said that my record would be cleared. He walked me to the door and wished me a good evening. When I got home I tried to heal my wounds. I had welts on my back and cuts on my arms. I made myself a steak dinner and opened a bottle of wine. I drank most of the bottle of wine until I convinced myself it was all a bad dream. The captain came by the next morning with a dozen red roses. He said he felt really bad about what had happened to me. "There was just so much going on at the station right now, there were bound to be some mistakes. Still, I hope you can find it in your heart to forgive us," he said. I took the roses from him and put them in a vase. "I've never really done anything to hurt anyone," I said. "I know that now. We were very much in the wrong. It makes me want to cry when I think of it," he said. "Well, it's over and I survived. I'm not going to sue anybody. I realize how difficult your job must be," I said. "We try our hardest, but every now and then we make a big mistake," he said. He was crying now, really sobbing. I went over and held him in my arms. "There, there, now," I said. He cuddled up to me. "I want my mommy," he said. "Don't we all," I said. "I want my teddy bear," he said. Then he fell asleep in my arms.

Dome of the Hidden Temple

People were going about their chores. Some were eating
lunch. Others, like me, were just standing around doing nothing,
just taking in the scene. I saw a dozen ducks fly over low
on their way to the pond. A policeman walked by swinging his
club. The firemen were washing their fire truck. Margie walked
out of a shoe store and saw me. She walked up to me and said,
"Have you heard the news? Rosie and Larry broke up." "Why?
They were the best darn couple I knew," I said. "I agree.
They had everything going for them," she said. "Did you talk
to her?" I said. "She says he thinks he's an armadillo. He
eats insects and mud and dug a burrow in back of the house,"
she said. "He didn't look like an armadillo. I thought he was
a very good-looking guy, always very nice to me," I said. "Whatever
the case, I'll miss their parties. They were always such fun,"
she said. "They were the best," I said. "I've got to run. Nice
to see you, Tim," she said. I walked over to the drugstore and
bought myself some toothpaste. When I came out, a light spring
rain had started. The pigeons on the bank took off and flew in
circles around the town. A man walked up to me and said, "Do
you know where the Dome of the Hidden Temple is?" I said, "Yes,
but I can't tell you. It's a secret." "But I'm supposed to meet
somebody there," he said. "Then that person should have told
you how to get there," I said. "I guess he thought I knew," he
said. "Almost nobody knows," I said. "Then why do you know?"
he said. "Because I am the Priest of Nothingness," I said.
"Are you really?" he said. "No, I just made that up," I said.
"Oh, so you're a comedian," he said. "Yes, I'm a comedian," I
said. "Well, you're not very good," he said. "I know," I said.

A Walk in the Woods

Down a little dusty street in the middle of nowhere a boy walked. He wore a baseball cap and carried a walking stick. He was trying to whistle a tune, but nothing came out. A toad sat on a stump and watched him. The boy thought he knew where he was, but wasn't sure. The road turned into a dirt road, and now he thought he was lost. His mother thought he was playing with a friend. He wasn't sure what had driven him here, only that he liked walking alone. Tall pines loomed on either side. A woodpecker was working on one of them. Tommy stopped and looked into the woods. Nothing could be seen, but shadows flitted back and forth and he felt certain there must be something there. There was a pond on the right on which a few ducks floated. He stopped to watch. He thought he saw a head floating on the surface, but it was just a shadow. The pond was full of shadows. He skipped a stone across the pond. Then turned and walked on down the road. There was a small boarded-up cabin on his left. Tommy walked past and into the darkness the trees provided. He felt like he was being watched. He stopped and looked around. Then he decided to walk back. The ducks were still in the pond, but there was something else. It looked like a human head. He looked closer and saw that it was just a bunch of tangled-up roots. Still, his heart was beating faster. He started to run. He tripped and fell and lay there bleeding. A man stood there and said, "My poor, poor child."

My Home

Down by the railroad tracks I found an old man asleep. I sat down beside him and waited for him to wake. A freight train went by with a hundred and thirty-six cars. I know. I counted them. Eventually, he woke up. He said, "Who the hell are you?" "I might be your friend, I don't know," I said. "I don't have friends," he said. "Okay, let's start someplace else. I'm not your enemy. How's that?" I said. "Okay, what do you want from me then?" he said. "I just want to chat," I said. "About what?" he said. "About your life," I said. "Well, that's a great story," he said. "Tell it to me, if you would," I said. "Well, I was born in Akron, Ohio. I had three older brothers and a sister. My father died when I was three. I dropped out of high school when I was a sophomore," he said. "You want more?" "Yes, give me more," I said. "I worked as a paperboy for two years, then started my own newspaper," he said. "I ran that for five years." "What made you stop?" I said. "I ran out of money. My debts were too great, I couldn't pay them off," he said. "What did you do then?" I said. "I discovered the rails. That was the life for me from then on," he said. "You rode the rails for thirty years?" I said. "No, I slept beside them," he said. "You never left Akron?" I said. "Akron's my home. Why would I leave it?" he said.

Manual for Self-Improvement

It was the first day of my life. That's what I told my-
self. I walked over the bridge of contentment and followed
the path of self-possession. The first man I met punched me
in the mouth and I saw stars, and the blood running down my
throat. I said, "Did I say something to offend you?" He said,
"You're full of shit, that's all." "Excuse me, I have no memory
of our having met before," I said. "We haven't, I just wanted us
to get off to a good start. I know your type and I can't stand
them," he said. "And what type is that?" I said. "You think
you're better than everybody else. You're smug, that's what
you are," he said. "You're wrong about that. I'm very humble,"
I said. He spit on me, then walked away into the trees. I sat
there twiddling my thumbs until a large hawk flew over. I
could see that it held a mouse in its talons. "Good-bye, little
mouse," I said. "I'm just going for a little ride. I'll be
back, trust me," it said. I waved to him and he was gone. I
stood up and walked for a while. I came to a lake, which was
just a glass of water on an abandoned beach. I dove in anyway
and swam around for some minutes until I banged my head on the
side of the glass. I climbed out and shook my head. A bee
buzzed my nose. "Why are you doing that?" I said. "Oh, excuse
me, I thought you were a tulip," it said, then flew off. I didn't
know I looked like a tulip. Well, maybe when wet. I walked a
little further. Nothing looked familiar. I was in a strange
land. There was a bamboo curtain behind which sat a little
mouse. "Hello, friend," he said. I looked again. He wasn't
there. And, then, neither was I.

Plans to Destroy the World

I sat at my desk most of the afternoon. What I did there I don't know. I scribbled and took some notes. Hours went by with little notice. When I woke I made some dinner. Something was wrong. I ate my dinner and went for a walk. My head kept spinning. Along the way I saw a hawk circling overhead. I wondered what he saw down here. It took my mind off my own problems. But, then, after a while, it was gone. It was getting dark and I headed back home to my worries and problems. When I got there the door was open. I called hello through the hallway. No answer. Then I crept in, peeking around corners. When I got to the kitchen, a man grabbed me by the collar and said, "Where is it?" "Where is what?" I said. "You know what I'm after. Give it to me now," he said. "Honestly, I don't know what you're looking for," I said. "You know," he said. "No I don't," I said. "Well, you better start thinking," he said. I tried to think of what he could want, but I came up with nothing. "I want your notes on the bomb. Now stop messing with me. Where's your desk?" he said. I took him to my desk. He grabbed the sheets off of the top of my desk. "This must be it!" he said. He looked at me intensely. "It's all here, isn't it?" I hesitated. "Yes, sir, it's all there, every bit of it," I said. "I guess I should say thank you. But thieves aren't supposed to say that. I should tie you up, I guess, but I won't. I'll just say good-bye," he said. And with my scribbles under his arm he dashed to the front door. I didn't even report him to the police.

Invisible

A man walked out of the post office, walked down the steps, and spoke to me. I didn't know the man, but spoke to him anyway. He got into a yellow car and drove away. Later that week I was at the dump. I was just about to throw a big box of books away when the same man said to me, "Don't do that. There's good reading in there." I gave the box to him. A month later I was standing on the street corner downtown thinking about something when the same man walked up to me and said, "Which way do you want to go?" I said, "I wasn't really thinking about going anywhere. I was just thinking." "Well, you could think at my house. My house is made for thinking," he said. "Oh, no thanks, I'm doing just fine right here. I like to think on street corners," I said. I forgot all about him after that. I met him a year later at a Christmas party. I heard a yell clear across the way and I looked up. I could never forget his face, all smiles. "Chester," he said. How did he know my name? "What a surprise to see you here." "I've been here every year for the past fifteen years," I said. "Well, I've been here for twenty," he said. "But I've never seen you here before," I said. "Maybe one of us is invisible," he said. I thought he was joking, but then I turned around and he was gone. Oh, well, I thought, I didn't like him anyway.

The Chicago Dead

The people on the bus all seemed to be foreigners. I
spoke to one of them and he just stared back at me as if I
were speaking gibberish. When I got off I waved to them good-bye.
They all stared into space. I started walking. I walked past
the 5 & 10. I walked past the statue of Thomas Jefferson, and
then past the Oliphant Bridge. There was no one on the street.
I got to the park and there was no one there. This had never
happened before. I walked to the merry-go-round, and gave
myself a push. I went around twice, then jumped off. It was
no fun. I walked back up to the street and saw another bus go
by. It was full of corpses, I was sure of it! Then, across the
street, I saw a man dart into a building. I ran after him. When
I got to the building I wasn't sure what to do. It was an apart-
ment building and how was I to know which apartment he went into?
I started up the stairs and pounded on each door as I passed.
At the very top a man answered. "What can I do for you?" he
said. "I saw you outside. What do you think is going on?" I
said. "Nothing's going on, nothing different from any other day,"
he said. "You didn't see all those dead people? And the streets
are empty, there's nobody anywhere," I said. "I saw lots of people,
they're everywhere," he said. "Oh, I'm sorry, you must be from
another universe," I said. "No, I'm from Chicago," he said.
"Are there lots of dead people there?" I said. "Yes, but we keep
them all underground," he said. "That's cruel," I said. "No,
we let them out on Easter morning," he said.

iii.

The Little Green Man

The rain fell all day and I was in a terrible mood. I gen-
erally like the rain so it made no sense to me. I guess things
were just going lousy for me. I threw up after breakfast. Don't
ask me why. And then I fell down the steps going to work. I
didn't break anything as far as I know. When I got to work I called
Janice Bob and she slapped me. Things went pretty well until
lunch. I ordered calamari and they brought me a rattlesnake.
I tried to be polite, but how do you eat a rattlesnake? I couldn't
eat it. When the waiter came at the end of the meal he saw that
I hadn't eaten anything. He said, "You didn't like your calamari?"
I said, "This doesn't look like the calamari I had in mind." "This
is western calamari," he said. "I like eastern," I said. I went
back to the office after lunch. There was a note on my door that
said, "You're next." That's all. I started quivering in my shoes.
Who had I offended? Only Janice, and she wouldn't kill anybody.
I started looking in my desk for something to defend myself with.
All I came up with was a stapler. I could knock the gun or knife
out of his hand with my right hand and staple his left hand to his
forehead. Just then there was a knock on my door. It was my boss.
He said, "I said you're next." I relaxed. "Yes, sir," I said.
I went into his office unarmed. He said, "Jack, I wanted you to
know that I think you're doing a terrific job, but, in spite of that,
I'm going to have to let you go. We have to tighten our belt."
I left his office, gathered my stuff, and drove home. I opened
the door and a little green monster jumped out at me. No he didn't.
He just stood there and stared.

Rats

The church bell rang at noon every day and we all scurried home for lunch. There were six of us, Mama and Poppa, Henry and David, Betsy and me. We had forty-five minutes to eat. One day there was a rat in the stew. Mama tried to hide it, but we found out. Poppa said to throw it all out, but Henry and David said no, then we wouldn't have anything to eat. Betsy said she wouldn't eat it, it would make her sick. I said I didn't care. Poppa said there would be no lunch today, that we would have to go back to work hungry and starve until dinner. I said I would be weak. Henry and David agreed. Betsy said she'd rather be weak than dead. And so we all went to work weak and struggled through our day. I started hallucinating around 4:00 and barely made it home alive. "What's for dinner?" were my first words in the door. "Wait till the others get here," Mama said. Henry and David were home shortly. And then, finally, Betsy. We sat around the dinner table eagerly waiting. Finally, Mama came out with a platter of roast chicken. We all applauded and Poppa started carving. We all got what we wanted. We said our prayers and started eating. We ate so much we were stuffed. Then Henry and David started to get sick. Then Betsy, too. Poppa came over and patted me on the head. "You're a tough one, just like your Ma and Pa. You're going to inherit this farm. You've got to eat rats to survive," he said.

The Waterfall

Brenda and I were taking a Sunday drive in the country.
"Is there any place you'd especially like to go?" I asked her.
"Let's go see the waterfalls over by Bernardston," she said.
So we drove over there and parked beneath the falls. It was a
beautiful waterfall, but after a while there isn't much to see.
So I said, "Are you ready to move on?" She said, "Sure." So
I started the engine and, just as I was about to leave, a barrel
rolled over the falls. I said, "What's that?" She said, "It's
just an old barrel." "Maybe there's someone in it," I said.
"I don't think so. It's just an old barrel," she said. "No,
I think there may be somebody in it," I said. "What makes you
think that?" she said. "What would an old barrel like that
be doing out on a lake?" I said. "Okay, so what are you going to
do?" she said. "I had better dive in and rescue it," I said.
"This seems absurd to me," she said. "I'm going after it before
it's too late," I said. I leapt out of the car, took off my
shoes, and dove in. I swam out to the barrel and pushed it
to the other shore. I grabbed a rock and started bending the
nails that had kept the lid in place. When I removed the lid
there was a little old lady crouched on the bottom. She said,
"Please help me out of here." I said, "How did you get in here?"
She said, "I have no idea. I was taking a nap at home, and the
next thing you know I was going over the falls." I said, "Well, who do
you live with?" She said, "I live with no one. And I always keep
my doors locked." "That's very peculiar. Did anyone want to do
you harm?" I said. "I have no enemies, as far as I know of,"
she said. And so we drove her home. "That was quite exciting.
That was the most fun I've had in years," she said. We said
good-bye and promised we'd visit again soon. She said, "It was
you, wasn't it?" I said, "I wasn't sure, but maybe it was."

The Mule

Someone rode by, but I don't know how, because I had my
head hidden behind a rock in the field. When they were gone
I stood up and brushed myself off. I looked over my shoulder
and saw the horse disappearing into the canyon. I didn't know
who the rider was, but I suspected it might be one of the
McKenzie boys. I had known Arthur since I was a boy, but we
hadn't spoken in many years. It wasn't anything official, just a
fact of life. I started running, as if I were being chased.
It felt good. I had been hiding behind that rock for a long time.
I ran down the brook, leapt over it, and ran up the long hill. I
stood there looking. Way off in the distance I saw a mule.
I ran toward it. I don't know why the mule interested me.
It didn't really. It was just to have a destination. So I
tried to keep him in view. Then I went down into a gully and
when I came up the mule was gone. A mule can't move that fast,
so I was confused. There was the same tree and the same wheel-
barrow, but the mule was gone. Finally, when I got there I
looked everywhere, but there was no mule. I called out for him,
but he wasn't there. It made no sense to me. I walked around
and looked for him everywhere. There was no mule anywhere.
I sat down on the ground and wept. Maybe there had never been
a mule there. No, that was impossible. I had definitely seen
a mule. I had followed it all the way here. I said, "Where are
you, mule?" A voice said, "I'm behind you. I have always been
behind you." I said, "You're not a mule. You're a man dressed
as a mule." He said, "You can't have everything you want, can
you? I'm almost as good."

Mimi and the Bear

I was sweeping up in the basement after a flood when I
thought I heard someone knocking on the kitchen door upstairs.
I put down the broom and ran up the stairs and opened the door.
It was Chet. "I hope I'm not interrupting anything important,
but I was in the neighborhood and I thought I'd drop by," he
said. "I was just sweeping the basement. Come on in," I said.
I got us some sodas and we went out on the porch to sit. "Mimi's
left me. She's gone home to Idaho to be with her mother," he said.
"Jesus, I'm sorry. I thought you two were the best couple I
knew," I said. "We were very good together for a long time. I
don't know what happened. I guess we got too used to each other,"
he said. "I really liked Mimi. Maybe she'll come back," I
said. "She has friends out in Idaho. She can probably get a
job," he said. "How are you holding up?" I said. "I think I
knew it was going to happen. I've been preparing myself," he
said. "Good. It's important to carry on. It takes a while,
but the pain will fade and you'll be yourself again," I said.
"There's a bear looking in your window over there," he said.
"He comes almost every day in the summer. I think he wants me
to let him in the house. He's curious to see how we live," I
said. "You aren't going to let him in, are you?" he said.
"Of course not. I'm not a fool," I said. "He looks sad, doesn't
he?" "Yes, but he could still kill you in a second," I said.
"Mimi was like that," he said.

Black Widow

I said that I knew someday a giant snake was going to eat us all. Monica poked at her tapioca. "There's something in here, something's moving," she said. "I'm going to Alaska. I want to make a man out of myself before it's too late," Wayne said. "A grizzly bear has written a book. Somebody told me that. Anyway, it's not very good. It's all about salmon fishing and how lonely that is," Harvey said. "I've read it. I like books about fishing," Roberta said. "On a day like today I could jump in the ocean and swim like a fish. I could take off all my clothes," Alex said. "You could be swallowed by a whale. Lots of people disappear like that," Kate said. "They travel around like that for years, and then they come back. They don't know anything because it was dark in there, so they cry all the time," Bob said. "I was kidding about the giant snake," I said. "How did this spider get into my tapioca? Oh my God, I think it's a black widow. Somebody's trying to kill me," Monica said. "It is a black widow. It means you've been chosen for some horrible job, but what could that be?" Wayne said. "Perhaps you've been chosen to wash the dishes," Harvey said. "I read a book about black widows once. They're really very nice," Roberta said. "Isn't somebody going to kill it?" Alex said. "It's bad luck to kill a black widow spider. They climb inside your soul and gnaw on it for years until there's nothing left," Kate said. Bob swatted it with a newspaper. "It's a beautiful spring day. Why don't we take a walk? The sun's out, the birds are singing," he said. We all looked at him as if he were insane. "Bob, this is a business meeting. We have much work to do. Singing birds are all very nice, but they won't map the charts or dodge the collapse of our empire, will they?" I said. "We won't know until we give them a try," he said. "The spider's moving," Monica said. Bob put his cigarette out on it.

The Suspect

One night I was standing on my front porch smoking a
cigarette and having a drink when I heard a loud explosion
down the street. I ran out into the street to have a look,
but could see nothing. I started walking down the street
slowly, looking around for a puff of smoke or anything.
A girl walked out of one of the houses and started up the
street. I stopped and stared at her, and then began
to follow her. She slowed once to look over her shoulder,
and I froze. Then she went on. I had no reason to believe
she was connected to the explosion, it's just that she
looked like someone who would be fun to follow. That's not
true. I don't know why I said that. She wore a dark hat
pulled low over her eyes, and a black trench coat with the
collar turned up. I couldn't even see her face. But then
she stopped. She turned around and said to me, "Why are
you following me?" "I thought maybe you set the bomb off
back there," I said. "What if I did? What business is it
of yours?" she said. "Oh, none, I suppose. Just curious,"
I said. "And you'd follow me all this way just out of
curiosity?" she said. "Just look at you, you look like
the lady who lit bombs," I said. "Well, I didn't. I'm just
back from visiting some gerbils," she said. "Relatives?"
I said. "No," she said, "just friends."

To Hell and Back

There was no flour left in the cupboard so I decided
to go to the store in spite of the storm. I put on all my
rain gear and headed out. It was only a short walk to the
store. A man stopped me along the way and said, "Which way
is the Grand Canyon?" "I have no idea. It's not around
here," I said. "I thought sure it was just around the
corner," he said. We walked on and on in the rain, and
suddenly there was the Grand Canyon. "I never knew it was
so close," I said. "I thought it was closer," he said. A
man in rags offered to rent us some donkeys and we accepted.
We rode them down a steep gulch and the sun came out and it
was 110. We rode on and on and my head began to be dizzy.
Buzzards circled above us expecting us to drop dead any
minute. When night came we made camp. My companion, whose
name was Foreman, gathered some dead wood, and we made
a fire. He produced some beans and we had dinner. When we
woke up in the morning we were in my bed. I said, "What
are we doing here?" He said, "I got your flour."

The Cookie

I was sleeping on the couch when I heard a light
knocking on the door. It could have been the wind, but
I went to see anyway. I opened the door and who was standing
there but my mother, dead these past eight years. I said,
"Mother, how nice to see you. What a surprise." She said,
"Jack, I've been thinking. I was so wrong to spank you when
you were eight. I feel so bad about it." I said, "I don't even
remember it." "We were in Ma's Grocery Store. I thought
you stole a cookie from her cookie jar and I spanked you.
Then Ma told me she had given it to you. I felt so bad,"
she said. "But, Mother, I don't even remember it," I said.
"That's all there is," she said. "Can I get you a glass
of tea?" I said. She started to fade. "Mother," I said,
"don't go. We have so much else to talk about, please."
But she was gone. But wait a minute, it's coming back to
me. I did steal the cookie but Ma wanted Mother to stop
spanking me. That Ma was a saint. But Mother shouldn't
give up so much time of her eternal rest over such a small
thing as a cookie.

The Green Shutters

As I remembered it, there was an oak tree in front of the house. Now, there was no oak tree. In fact, there was no house. Just an empty plot of ground was all that was left. Oh, there were neighbors on both sides of where the house used to be, but their memories were gone, and an open space is all they remember. We no longer existed, or we never existed is more like it. I decided to test my theory. I went up to my neighbor on the left and knocked on the door. An old woman answered, a Mrs. Steinhauser as I recalled, and I asked her if she remembered the Brennans. She said no she didn't, in fact she had never heard of the name. I said my name was John Brennan and I grew up in the house next door, now demolished. She stared at me. I said, "I know you from my childhood." She looked at me as though I were trying to sell her a faulty parachute. "You used to sell us rutabagas from your garden." "I'm sorry, but I don't remember you," she said. "We had a dog named Fred you said dug in your garden," I said. "I don't remember any dog," she said. "I mowed your lawn one summer," I said. "I don't remember that," she said. "The next summer I painted your shutters green. You must remember that," I said. "I remember green shutters," she said. "Well, Mrs. Steinhauser, I'm glad you remember those green shutters even though you don't remember me. We spent ten years next to your house and now we are just shadows flitting about the pavement. How would you feel in our shoes?" I said. "Good-bye, Mr. Brennan," she said as she shut the door. I looked at her door, then over at our yard. An emu was grazing in the pastures.

Love at First Sight

One night I got off early from work and decided to stop
by the tavern on the way home. Tommy and Johnny and Strike
were there, Strike and Tommy were playing pool. Johnny and
I sat at the bar talking with the owner. His marriage had
just broken up and we were trying to comfort him. "You must
meet a lot of women in the bar," Johnny said. "Well, you do,
but they're not really women you would want to take home,"
he said. "I know what you mean," Johnny said. "Maybe for
one night," I said. They both laughed. Tommy and Strike
finished their game and joined us. "How about a couple of
beers?" Strike said to the owner. The owner, Joe, reached
for the spout, clutched his heart, and fell to the ground.
Johnny and I screamed. Tommy jumped over the bar and grabbed
the phone and called an ambulance. Joe was in the hospital
a week. We visited him once. He had had open heart surgery.
But he was in good shape. He introduced us to his nurse.
When he got out he was back at the bar, but he was quieter.
One night when I was in there by myself he told me, "I've
met the girl of my dreams. You won't believe how sweet she is."
"Who's that?" I said. "You'll just have to wait and see," he said.
A couple of months went by. One night I was in there pretty
much by myself and he said, "Do you want to come over to my
place Wednesday night?" So I went. When I got there I was
surprised to find the place all lit up in candles. There
were a few other guests, not people from the bar. And in the
living room there was a casket with the corpse all laid out
in a bridal gown. "I met her at the hospital," Joe explained.
"It was love at first sight."

Dreaming

Kindred spirits like ours never fall apart, I always told myself. We skied, we hiked, we ran, we loved lavish dinners, we loved to sing. We loved to talk late into the night. So, when she got sick we were both caught quite off guard. The doctor said she might not live for long. I tried to take care of her the best I could, but, the truth is, I got bored. One night I suggested we sing, but she said she was tired. A week later I suggested that I take her on a boat ride. She thought about it, but said she might feel like it in a week or so. I was getting impatient or bored. I went on a bike ride by myself. The flowers were beautiful all along the path. When I came back she was sleeping. The next day Tom and Alice invited us to dinner. I discussed it with Colleen. She said I must go by myself. I went and had a fine time. When I got home I wanted to talk about it with Colleen, but she was asleep. I started to hike by myself. I'd see wild animals and never tell Colleen. I kept it all to myself. But then she started to get better, or so it seemed. We started to take short walks together. I fixed our favorite dinner. I put her to bed and sat up dreaming of our life together. The next morning I woke and made her breakfast. When I took it in she was gone, I mean she was dead. I stood there looking at her. She was so beautiful. She said, "Hank, I'm only dreaming."

What Are Worms?

I fled down the drainpipe and then over the two hills behind the house. My wife came chasing after me. When she caught me we fell into a hole. "What are you doing here?" I asked. "I wanted to know where you were going," she said. "This hole was not my intention," I said. "I'm sure it wasn't," she said. "Now what are we going to do?" I said. "We can either try to make ourselves comfortable or try to find a way out," she said. "A way out would be nice," I said. "Why don't I climb on your back?" she said. "Why don't I climb up on yours?" I said. "Because you're the stronger," she said. "Why don't we just make ourselves at home?" I said. "There's no television," she said. "We could carve something into the wall," I said. "But it wouldn't move," she said. "And neither would we," I said. "That's what I call a restful afternoon," she said. "Almost dead," I said. "Not quite," she said. "Why is that?" I said. "I have a cookie in my head," she said. "You have a cookie in your head?" I said. "Yes, I have a cookie in my head," she said. "If we just had a glass of milk we could have a party," I said. "But I don't have any milk," she said. "Do I look like a cow?" "Most certainly not. You look like you're my wife," I said. "But what are we doing in this hole?" she said. "We're worms, aren't we?" I said. "No, we certainly are not," she said. "Then I don't know," I said.

The Flag

The flag was still there. No, it wasn't. What am I talking
about? We didn't even have a flag. This was after the war.
Nobody had a flag. We didn't even have anything to eat. We wore
rags. We roamed the streets like zombies gathering scraps for
our babies and old people. Every once in a while we'd come upon
a turkey or a duck and we'd descend on it like savages; I mean,
a picture of a turkey or a duck. There were no such real animals
left. We'd sit around the campfire and talk about the old days.
Mostly nobody remembered any. Somebody would say, "Remember when
we used to play baseball in the park?" And there would be a dead
silence. Enoy, a former mailman, would say, "I remember every-
thing, baseball, football, you name it." And Griselle, a former
model, would say, "I don't remember anything. It's like this is
the only thing I have ever experienced, hunger and searching for
something I never had." "Now, now," Granny said, "times have
been worse." "Tell me when," Ben said. "In my youth they were
worse, I'll tell you that," Granny said. "Well, I wasn't there,
so I can't say," Ben said. They would talk like that until the
last embers were sputtering. In the morning we would start search-
ing again. Someone found an old burning tire. Another found a
dead crow. "Things are looking good," someone said. "Better than
yesterday," another said. "I found a flag," I said. "That's
really great," Enoy said. "Just kidding," I said.

Where the Money Is

"What if I never see you again?" I said. "Oh, you will. One of these days I'll walk right back into your life," he said. It was hard to believe that exchange took place twenty years ago. Jack was my best friend at the time, but he grew vague over time. I got married and ten years later got divorced. Then I had a girlfriend for five years. I got promoted at the office. I was doing pretty well for myself. Then one day Jack showed up. He had a beard and so on, but I recognized him. I said, "You old son-of-a-bitch, you kept your word. It's twenty years, just like you said." "I told you I'd be here, and here I am," he said. "Well, come on in. Tell me what you've been up to," I said. We sat down in the living room and I got us something to drink. "Now tell me all about yourself," I said. "Well, there isn't much to tell. I joined the army when I was nineteen. I fought in Korea for a while. When I got out I went to Montana and shepherded for a couple of years. When I had enough money I bought some land in Wyoming. And that's when I started raising cattle. Before long I had a couple of hundred. But then the drought came along and I lost them all. I didn't know what to do," he said. "What did you do?" I said. "Well, I drank for a spell. Then I started digging a hole in my backyard. I dug and I dug until I finally came across a dinosaur skeleton, complete, I mean it was huge. I cleaned it all off and sold it to the Natural History Museum in New York City for a million bucks," he said. "My God, what did you do then?" I said. "Well, I invested it all in oil and the well went bust," he said. "What luck!" I said. "And what are you doing now?" "I'm sweeping the halls of a junior high school,"

he said. "What a life!" I said. "I've never been happier,"
he said. "Why do you suppose that is, Jack?" I said. "These
little kids are going to grow up to be dinosaurs," he said.
"They're disappearing. They're going underground." "And you're
going to dig them up," I said. "Exactly," he said.

For Rent

I sat there in the train station looking everyone over
from head to toe. I was looking for one particular person,
though I didn't know who that was. There was an old man
wearing a bowtie and white shoes who seemed mightily suspicious,
but then he left the station without turning around. And then
there was a young woman who dropped her hankie by my shoe
and neglected to pick it up. I was just about to leave when
two young boys came skipping across the auditorium
and started wrestling with one another on the floor not too
far in front of me. One of them beat the other one's head
on the floor and knocked him out. He got up and left shortly
after that. I went over and checked on the other one. He
wasn't breathing. I pounded on his chest. I looked in his
eyes. He wasn't human. He was a doll, a very big doll. I
stood up and brushed my collar and went to get myself a
lemonade. As I was standing there drinking a man walked
up to me and said, "You don't want your dummy?" "Oh, that's
not mine. I was just visiting it," I said. "You were just
visiting a dead dummy?" he said. "Say, you look familiar,"
I said. "I rent the dead dummies," he said.

The Grandmother

　　I was walking down the street with a laundry bag over
my shoulder when a kid stopped me and said, "What do you have
in that bag, mister?" "My grandmother is in this bag," I said.
"Why?" he said. "She was acting real bad last night, and I
hit her with a baseball bat," I said. "What are you going to
do with her?" he said. "I'm going to take her out in my boat
and drop her in the middle of the lake," I said. "Can I see
her?" he said. "No, she's a mess," I said. "I don't care,"
he said. "Her head's all bashed in," I said. "I've seen worse
in movies," he said. "Okay," I said, "give me a second." I
threw the bag on the ground and untied it. I opened it slowly.
It was full of white feathers. The boy said, "There's no grand-
mother there." "I don't understand. I swear she was there,"
I said. "You're playing a joke on me," he said. "No, she was
there, I swear it," I said. "Maybe she's gone to heaven and
become a saint," he said. "She was no saint," I said. "Maybe
she was a chicken," he said. "She wasn't a chicken," I said.
"How about a turkey?" he said. "Not a turkey," I said. He
thought for a while. "I've got it. An ostrich. She was an
ostrich," he said. "I think you're right. She was incredibly
fast. Her mouth was hard like a beak, and her arms were like
short short wings. She was an ostrich," I said. "What were you
doing with an ostrich as a grandmother?" he said. "I don't
know," I said.

The Furnace

The doctor told me to go home and get some rest. So
I went home and the furnace blew up. I called the repair-
man right away. A few hours later he came in his truck
and worked the rest of the day in the basement. When he
came up he was black with soot. "What do you think?" I
said. "I couldn't find it," he said. "What do you mean
you couldn't find it? You look like you've been inside of
it for hours," I said. "Well, I was, but when I came out
it was nowhere in sight. It was completely gone," he said.
"But look at you. You've been somewhere dark and dirty,"
I said. "Dark and dirty, that's a nice way to put it,"
he said. "Well, how would you put it?" I said. "Black
lace," he said. "Black lace? I don't think I know what
you mean," I said. "There are roads everywhere and none
of them will get you out," he said. "But how did you get
out?" I said. "I never said I was in," he said. "I don't
understand," I said. "Neither did I," he said.

Llamas

One night I thought I saw a llama cross the road. When I got home I called the police. "There's no llamas that live around here," he said. "But I saw one tonight," I said. "That's what we call a hallucination," he said. "Thank you for the information," I said. I never saw a llama after that, but other people did. Mother came over to visit one day. She wore a pink hat. I said, "Mother, what a lovely hat." She said, "It's part llama." I said, "Which part?" "I don't know, they didn't tell me," she said. Later, that evening, after she had left, I found a pair of keys beneath the sofa. I thought they might be hers so I called her. No one answered so I forgot about it. A week passed and I didn't hear from her, which was not unusual. But after two weeks I began to wonder. I went over to her place and found it locked. I looked all around, for what I don't know. I called the police. They said she had probably gone on vacation. I said she would have told me. I called her every day to no avail. Then I got a postcard from South America. She was traveling with a tribe of Indians and a large herd of llamas. They were headed for Paraguay, where they were to meet up with a couple of Third Reich officers. They were going to take over the world.

The Afterlife

        A man fell out of the tree in our backyard. I ran over
to help him. "Would you like some tea?" I said. "I think
I broke my back," he said. "Perhaps some ice cream would
be just the thing," I said. "Lend me your hand," he said.
I gave him my hand and tried to pull him up. When he was
upright, he said, "Where am I?" "You're in my backyard," I
said. "It's like nothing I've ever seen before," he said.
"It's just an ordinary yard, a small garden, a few flowers,"
I said. "Yes, it's a sorry sight. How can you stand to live
here?" he said. "Oh, it's my home," I said. "Home? That's
a curious word," he said. "Where do you live?" I said. "Live?
Live? That's a funny question," he said. "I don't live anywhere."
"What do you mean?" I said. "I'm a dead man. I just float
around," he said. "Well, I've never met a dead man. I'm
pleased to meet you," I said. "I think you're supposed to
scream or something," he said. "Oh no, I'm really pleased,"
I said. "It's really kind of you to drop by." "I didn't
drop by. It was the wind," he said. "And then the wind stopped
and I fell into the tree." "How lucky for me," I said. "You'll
be going with me, of course, when I leave. You'll never be
coming back," he said.

The Hammer to the Rescue

This morning I got up and checked the mail. The mail comes early in these parts. There was a package from Wyoming. I took it inside to open it. There were these three little fingers, not human, mind you, but fingers nonetheless. Furry things and malleable, like you'd want to touch your face. Who sent these? There was no return address. I took them out of the box and began to juggle them in the air. One scratched my eye. Another clung to my wrist. And the third one just kept dancing in the air as if that were the normal thing to do. Then I put them back into their box. The box kept rattling. I put it in my top dresser drawer and left the room. I fixed myself some breakfast, washed the dishes. I went out onto the front porch and smoked a cigarette. My neighbor came over and asked me if he could borrow a hammer. I said sure and we walked back to the shed. We talked for a while, about the World Series, about gophers, murderers, saints. I liked Joe. He was a good sort. We walked back from the shed and I told him about the hairy fingers I received in the mail. He said he'd like to see them. So I took him into the house and into the bedroom. I opened the drawer of the dresser and carefully opened the box. There was nothing there. "You were just joshing me about those fingers, weren't you?" he said. "I swear I wasn't. I don't know where they've gone," I said. I felt something crawling up my back. Just as I was about to say something, one of the fingers stuffed itself into my mouth and the other two pressed down on my eyelids. Joe said, "What kind of joke is this?" I said, "Argh, argh." He took the hammer and hit me on the head. That's the last thing I remember.

The End of the Line

       The trolley stopped in front of the hardware store. I
got on and paid my fare. I found a seat by the window and stared
at the people on the sidewalk. A band walked by playing a tune
from a Broadway show. Several clowns were playing tricks with
balloons. A woman sat down next to me. She was loaded down with
packages. A police car passed us with its siren blaring. I said,
"Do you need help with all those packages?" "Oh no, my husband's
going to meet me at the end of the line," she said. "That's good,"
I said. Just then a very fat man got on the trolley and wobbled
down the aisle. He looked at each vacant seat very carefully, sizing
up his chances of fitting into it. When he got to the seats in front
of ours, both of which were empty, he sat down. He wiped the sweat
from his forehead with a hankie, then leaned back and snored. I
looked at my seatmate and smiled. She smiled back. The trolley
crossed a bridge and rattled. One of her packages fell to the
floor. I bent over and picked it up, rubbing her leg. "Sorry,"
I said. "That's all right," she said. Just then the fat man fell
out of his seat into the aisle. The man across the aisle from him
reached down and said, "He's dead!" "Stop the trolley!" someone
shouted. But the trolley went on. Several people gathered around
the fat man and tested his pulse. "He's dead all right," one of
them said. "Stop this trolley!" one man shouted. "We must get
him off of here," another said. "What's all the fuss," I said to
my seatmate, "he's dead." "I wish they'd just take us where we're
going," she said. Just as we crossed another bridge, the trolley
stopped. The conductor got up and walked back to where we were.
He opened the doors and said, "I'll need some help." Three men
got up and walked to where he was. "Now when I say three we'll all

give a shove," he said. They pushed him into the river. Then the trolley resumed its course until the end of the line, where my seatmate's husband greeted her and carried her packages. I waved good-bye.

The Dead Animal

The store was empty at that time of night. I
was about to lock up when a young woman entered. "Can
I help you?" I said. "I'm just looking," she said. "If
I can help you with anything just let me know," I said.
She kept looking way past closing. I kept an eye on her.
Finally, she said, "Would you mind trying this on for me? I
think you are the same size as my father." "Of course,
I would be happy to," I said. I put on the sport coat.
It fit perfectly. "It makes you old," she said. "I am
old," I said. "Not like that," she said. "Here, try
this one." I tried on the one held out to me. "You look
short," she said. "I am short," I said. "Not like that,"
she said. "Try this one." I tried the one she offered.
"It makes you look green," she said. "Well, I'm not green,"
I said. "One more," she said. She handed me a coat I
could swear was made of wolf. "I'm not going to try
that one on. It scares me," I said. "Oh please, it
would mean so much to me," she said. "Oh, all right," I
said. I pulled on the heavy, old thing. "Oh, you look
divine in it. It really suits you," she said. "This
ratty thing?" I said. "No, you look heavenly, really
you do," she said. "I feel like a dead animal," I said.
She cozied up to me. "Wait a minute," I said. "I can't
wait," she said, and threw her arms around me, kissing me.

Tenderizer

There was a man in the doorway when I passed. I didn't see him at first, but then, just as I passed, I noticed him. He was an ordinary-looking bloke, no tattoos, as far as I could see, no obscene jewelry, no sharp pokes of hair. He was looking straight ahead. I stopped and looked back at him. "What are you staring at?" he said to me. "I was just looking at you," I said. "I'm invisible, you can't see me," he said. "I can see you just fine," I said. "You need special glasses to see me," he said. "Well, I guess I've got them," I said. "Lucky you," he said. "Why are you invisible?" I said. "Why are you not?" he said. "That's a good question. I guess I never wanted to be," I said. "There you go." "But I can see you now without special glasses," I said. "That means you're one of me," he said. "I don't think so. It means you're a fake," I said. "Okay, so I'm not invisible. Let's just say that most people don't see me. Isn't that about the same?" he said. "Oh yes, now I see what you're saying. Say, would you like to have a bite to eat with me?" I said. "Did you say, would I like to bite you?" he said. "Never mind. I've got to get going," I said. "But I would like to bite you," he said. "Tough," I said. "Oh, I have my own tenderizer," he said. "Use it on yourself," I said, and waved good-bye over my shoulder.

The Invisible Alligators

A little bit down the road I met an old lady who greeted
me with a wave of her hankie. I said, "Where's your dog?
I thought you had a dog." "Oh no, I never had a dog. I had
a cat once, but he died," she said. "I must be thinking of
someone else," I said. "There is no one else," she said.
"What do you mean?" I said. "On this street, I am the only
one without a dog," she said. "Oh yes, of course you are,"
I said. "In fact, I'm the only one without an alligator,"
she said. "Now wait a minute, I've never seen an alligator
on this street," I said. "Oh, you haven't been looking," she
said. "Well, I wouldn't have to be looking very hard to
see an alligator, would I?" I said. "They would bite you," she
said. "How do you get around them?" I said. "Oh, I have my
moves. Besides, they know me," she said. "I've never seen
one," I said. "Oh, they're invisible," she said. "I see," I said.
"No you don't. I told you they were invisible,"
she said. "Yes, I understand. That's what I meant," I said.
"Oh, I see," she said. "How can you see if they're invisible?"
I said, just to drag the conversation on a little bit. "Never
mind," she said. "Ouch," I said, "he bit me." "Who bit you?"
she said. "I don't know," I said.

A Quiet Day on the Porch

I sat on the stoop and twiddled my thumbs. A car went by
with five teenagers in it, shouting and yelling about something.
Then a man walked by, a doctor perhaps, doing sums in his head,
or so I imagined. A couple of squirrels were playing tag beneath
the big elm tree. Otherwise, a quiet day on the porch. I fell
asleep. A dream about an ocean voyage. Two monkeys were
chasing one another across the deck. One of them slipped and fell overboard.
The other one stood and stared at the drowning one, then started
dancing a sad ballet by himself until he finally slipped and drowned
himself. The crowd started applauding until they finally woke me.
I said, "What?" A baby robin was chirping from the branch of the
elm. I stood up, looked around, and walked into the house. I made
myself a sandwich and sat down at the table to eat it. The cheese
kept squeezing out of my sandwich, until I finally grabbed it and
threw it on the floor. A mouse came out of the wall and started
eating it. I said, "Go away, mouse, or I'll kill you." The mouse
looked up at me and said, "Fat chance." And he dragged the cheese
away into the unseen folds of the wall. I finished the remains of
the sandwich and washed up. I walked out onto the porch and
waved at a neighbor who was pushing her baby carriage up the street. There
was a fire in the carriage, but the neighbor didn't seem to care.

Plastic Story

I had barely said my prayers when I felt a large insect crawl
over my face. I was afraid to move. When I opened my eyes
I saw it was a piece of plastic that had torn loose from
a project I was working on in the next room. But what had
torn it loose? I couldn't figure it out. I got up and walked
into the adjoining room. It was all there, except for this
little piece. There's no wind in the house. A piece of plastic can't
fly on its own. It can't turn corners. It can't just say there's
a face I'm going to land on and tickle. I walked to the kitchen
and poured myself a glass of whiskey. I thought about things
of an ethereal nature. Then I thought about ants, I thought
about mosquitoes, I thought about mice. None of them seemed
to work. Maybe the Virgin Mary. That seemed like a good idea.
Maybe she had misunderstood my prayer. I decided to have one
more shot, and then go back to bed. Just as I had poured myself
a shot, a piece of plastic covered my hand. It had just floated
there out of nowhere. I stared at it for a while, then I
delicately picked it off with my thumb and forefinger. I tossed
it onto the floor and scooted it with my foot under the chair,
out of sight. Some things don't deserve to be contemplated.
I drank the shot of whiskey and went back to bed. Needless to say
I couldn't sleep. I lay there imagining myself strangled by a
piece of plastic. But then it was real. I wasn't imagining it.
A piece of plastic had grabbed my throat and was strangling me.
I fought with all my might, but it was too late. I had never
done a thing to hurt that plastic.

About the Author

JAMES TATE was born in Kansas City, Missouri, in 1943. He is the author of seventeen books of poetry, including *Worshipful Company of Fletchers*, which won the National Book Award in 1994; *Selected Poems*, which won the Pulitzer Prize and the William Carlos Williams Award in 1991; and *The Lost Pilot*, which was selected by Dudley Fitts for the Yale Series of Younger Poets. He has also published a novel and a collection of short stories, as well as edited *The 1997 Best American Poetry Anthology*. His honors include a National Institute of Arts and Letters Award for Poetry, the Tanning Prize, the Pulitzer Prize, the National Book Award, and fellowships from the Guggenheim Foundation and the National Endowment for the Arts. He teaches at the University of Massachusetts in Amherst.